T A L K   B A C K !

Talk Back!

The Gay Person's Guide to Media Action

Lesbian and Gay Media Advocates

Boston: Alyson Publications

To the 100,000 strong
at the October 14, 1979
March on Washington
for Lesbian and Gay Rights,
we lovingly dedicate this book

Published as a paperback original by Alyson Publications, Inc., Boston.
First printing: September, 1982.

ISBN 0 932870 10 4

Contents

Acknowledgments

First, we acknowledge our debt to Bill Mulkern, the LAGMA member who helped turn this fantasy of "a book" into a reality by doing the initial research and writing. Jennifer Gilman and Marcie Hershman commented on this draft, while to David Peterson, Diane Greene and Sasha Alyson fell the task of revising it and preparing the final copy.

LAGMA's collective wisdom weaves throughout the book, as do the thoughts and efforts of our other present and past members including: Ronnie Allen (our first archivist), Lee Edelman, Joe Litvak, JoEllen Mancuso, Kevin McFadden, Eric Rofes, Ed Sams, H.M. Smith, and Raymond Hopkins, to whom we owe the nurturant atmosphere of our meetings. Special appreciation goes to Marion Thorlander who, in October 1979, got LAGMA started.

Thanks also to those people outside of LAGMA who read the first draft and supplied extensive comments: David Rothenberg, Jim Vetter and John Zeh.

We owe a debt of gratitude to the National Gay Task Force, and especially to Tom Burrows, for compiling and sending a wealth of information from their now out-of-print media manual, and for allowing us to use some of this material directly. This saved us many, many hours of research. New England War Tax Resistance gave us a grant to support additional research.

We want to make a special acknowledgment to the *Boston Globe*. Because we are a Boston group, examples from the *Globe* fill the book and we have been free with our criticisms. But the *Globe* has made many changes; we thank them for being receptive to our ideas and we appreciate their increasing use of the words "gay" and "lesbian" — legitimizing our struggle in a way that papers like the *New York Times* have not.

Finally, we thank the growing number of individuals whose letters of protest and praise are increasingly often to be found in publications ranging from *Whole Earth Times* and *Ebony* to *T.V. Guide* and *Time*. You are models to us all.

Introduction

Lesbian and Gay Media Advocates — a fancy name for a small group of people who got fed up. Fed up with media that too often either distort our lives, and thus add fuel to the fires of discrimination, or ignore us, and thus do nothing to counteract the prevailing misconceptions of what it means to be a gay man or lesbian.

Some of us had been activists for years; for others, attending a first LAGMA meeting was itself an act of courage. At our meetings, we could *share* the sense of outrage, analyze clippings, relate things we saw and heard on TV and radio, plan strategies. We started writing letters, we approached major media outlets (newspapers, local television and radio stations) to set up meetings.

In the process we learned a lot. We learned that there are many people in the media who *will* listen, who did grow in their understanding of discrimination against lesbians and gay men, and who want to do something about the media's role in this.

We also learned that it is painful to do this sort of work. Raising other people's consciousness takes a lot out of you. (And some people's misconceptions do not budge — we discovered that too.) One of the first things we had to learn was to *expect more*. It was that long-internalized self-hatred that had accounted for our passive acceptance of unacceptable media coverage — that and a belief that "they'll never change, why should we try to do anything about it?"

But we did try. And they did change.

Now we want you, too, to expect more. We want you to become a media activist, to do something about media coverage of our lives. We guarantee that putting your outrage into a letter will do more for your health than squashing, denying or internalizing that outrage.

Although this book is specifically concerned with media coverage of lesbians and gay men, many of our points and our strategies could easily be translated to the coverage afforded women, people of color, elders, and the physically and mentally disabled — in short, to any group of people whose lives are often trivialized, sensationalized, maligned or ignored by the media.

While we have tried to give enough information to make various facets of the media understandable, we have written this book mainly from our own experiences. Your experiences might differ; if so, we'd like to hear from you. Even if such differences exist, we hope they will not interfere with our major goal: to encourage lesbians and gay men to expect, to demand and to get fairer coverage of our lives in the media.

> Lesbian and Gay Media Advocates
> c/o Gay Community News
> P.O. Box 971
> Boston, Mass. 02103

1. The History of Media Work

Today when we see exceptionally distorted media coverage of lesbian and gay issues, it's easy to feel like the situation is hopeless. But actually we have made progress in the last thirty years, due mostly to the efforts of lesbians and gay men who have worked for better media coverage, and there's every reason to believe that progress can continue.

During the first half of the century, the subject of homosexuality was virtually untouched by the media. The average person could easily go through life without hearing anything more than an occasional oblique reference to "inverts" or "abnormal people."

The first breakthrough came when the Kinsey Report on male sexuality appeared in the late 1940s. It rapidly became the talk of the country; it was described as the fastest-selling and most talked-about book since *Gone With the Wind*. One of Kinsey's findings was widely quoted in coverage of the report: he said that 37% of American males have a homosexual experience after adolescence. Americans now realized that perhaps homosexuality was not confined to such a small, insignificant minority of the population.

Kinsey's report paved the way for the first truly positive discussion of homosexuality in the mainstream media. In 1949, an exchange of views on male homosexuality developed quite spontaneously in the letters pages of *Saturday Review*. These letters, including one by a self-identified gay man, are surprising in two ways. First, they are unprecedented. No other magazine or newspaper in the U.S. is known to have permitted such an open, public discussion of this subject. Second, most of the letters were as liberal as the times could allow. The writers all abhorred "flaunting"; they pointed out the great disparity between society's stereotypes and the real homosexuals the writers knew. They showed an acute awareness of the necessity and the limitations of the closet. They began to bring into the open subjects that had for too long been ignored.

It was an isolated and short-lived beginning. Soon the witch-hunts of the McCarthy era began, and thousands of government workers were fired because of their suspected homosexuality. Late in 1949 *Newsweek* ran the article "Queer People". It began: "The sex pervert, whether a homosexual, an exhibitionist, or even a dangerous sadist, is too often regarded merely as a 'queer' person who never hurts anyone but himself. . . ." The article never again referred to homosexuals; it went on to give examples of men murdering women and, in one case, a mother murdering her infant son. But the damage was done; to the average *Newsweek* reader, homosexuals were established as violent psychopaths.

It was in this atmosphere that the Mattachine Society was formed. Henry Hay, one of the founders, saw the country moving toward fascism and McCarthyism. He knew the target wouldn't be Jews — the Holocaust was too fresh in the nation's memory — or blacks, who were starting to organize. It would be homosexuals. The purpose of the Mattachine Society was "to unify isolated homosexuals. . . . to educate homosexuals and heterosexuals. . . . and to assist our people who are victimized daily as a result of our oppression."

One of the first attempts at gay media work came in 1952 when, in a three-page letter, the media was invited to attend the trial of Dale Jennings, an original Mattachine member who had been arrested on a solicitation change. Of course no media representatives attended, but at least a step had been made in trying to get fairer coverage of a gay man's life.

A successful lesbian organization was founded in 1955 by Del Martin and Phyllis Lyon. The Daughters of Bilitis (DOB) is still active today. Listed among its original purposes in 1955 was "the education of the public. . . leading to an eventual breakdown of erroneous taboos and prejudices."

One other development of the fifties was to have a far-reaching impact: television emerged as an important vehicle for shaping and reflecting public attitudes. While gay people constitute some 10% of the population, no one would have guessed that from the programming. Until 1972 no gay characters appeared on network television except for an occasional bizarre characterization of gay men. Lesbians were totally absent.

In the years 1972–74, that changed. Several shows tried to give a serious portrayal of homosexuality, though distortions and sensationalism were the rule. NBC ran the film "Born Innocent" and an episode of "Police Woman" that portrayed lesbians as brutal rapists and murderers.

Most famous was the episode of ABC's "Marcus Welby" in which a male science teacher rapes a male student. This resulted in the first organized nationwide protest by the gay movement for better media treatment. Members of the gay community met with representatives of the major networks, the Writers and Directors Guilds, and the Association of Motion Picture and Television Producers. The National Gay Task Force and others organized the Gay Media Task Force in Hollywood and, after much struggle, all three networks began consulting with this group about scripts involving gay men or lesbians.

In 1980, CBS aired a documentary about San Francisco's gay community, "Gay Power, Gay Politics", which merits special attention. The program focused on gay men to the exclusion of lesbians, and it used hearsay, exaggerations, and deceitful editing to distort its findings. It presented a picture of gay men as highly preoccupied with sex (especially S&M sex), unconcerned with public safety, and wielding a disproportionate amount of political power in San Francisco.

Gay men and lesbians everywhere were outraged by the

obvious bias and distortions of the show. Many phoned or wrote to CBS to complain. One person, San Francisco journalist Randy Alfred, went further. Alfred sought out documentation of the program's biases, then filed a 20-page complaint with the National News Council detailing 44 charges that, he said, "contribute to the cumulative effect of patterned distortion." The Council found that CBS had indeed been unfair in numerous respects. Although CBS never admitted to deliberate distortion, the pressure was finally enough to make it acknowledge these complaints on the air.

Thanks to the efforts of people like Randy Alfred, the networks today are less likely to present such stereotyped or negative images. Sometimes they'll even take a step forward: an episode of "All in the Family" did portray Edith Bunker's coming to terms with the fact that her recently deceased cousin had been a lesbian. In another show actress Jane Alexander gave a moving portrayal of a lesbian mother fighting for custody of her children.

But overall, positive gay male characters are still rare, and lesbians are even rarer in network programming. One TV writer tells of a story line he submitted for "The Senator", concerning whether a man should be considered a security risk because he was gay. The network rejected the script; the writer feels that was because "the treatment of the homosexual in my story was sympathetic and he was portrayed as neither nance nor psychopath."

The situation with the print media is somewhat different. Although newspapers get much of their material from the national wire services, their editorial policy is determined locally. Just as with TV and radio, newspaper coverage of gay issues is getting better wherever there are people pushing for it to improve.

In Boston, the Lesbian and Gay Media Advocates (LAGMA) was formed after the October 1979 March on Washington for Lesbian and Gay Rights, attended by some 100,000 people. Many of us came back to Boston expecting to see some prominent stories about this major news event; instead, the story was buried in the middle of the paper. It also grossly underestimated the size of the crowd and did not report on the several thousand Massachusetts residents who participated. Several of us were outraged enough to meet with editors from Boston's major newspapers and TV stations, to talk about how gay news could be sensitively and accurately covered, and to suggest stories that they could do about our community. These meetings, letter-writing, and work with the local lesbian and gay community to push for better coverage, *have* shown results. They're not always dramatic, not without an occasional step backward as well as forward, but clearly things are getting better. Moreover, we now have contacts at most of the major media. When a distorted story appears, or if we see something we think should get coverage, we can phone the appropriate person knowing that, while they may not do what we want, they at least will take us seriously.

If you are a lesbian or gay man, chances are you've read or heard something in the last few weeks that made you cringe. It may have been an announcer's articulation of "ho-mo-sexual" in a way that made it sound like a disease; a stereotyped image of our lives; a talk show guest's casual imitation of a "fag"; a sensational headline in the newspaper. You cringe, swallow it, and go on, figuring perhaps "that's the way it is — there's nothing I can do. They (the media) are ignorant, will never understand the breadth of the issues, will never change."

But across the country, groups and individuals *are* starting to monitor the media and push for improvements. Have you noticed, for example, that letters to the editor in *T.V. Guide* and other widely read magazines and news-papers do now contain occasional letters from angry lesbians and gay men about distortions and omissions?

We hope that after reading this book, you too will be ready and willing to talk back.

2. Introduction to the Media

In order to deal effectively with the media, you need to understand the functions the media perform, how the media are organized, and how they interact with each other.

The media with which we have the most direct contact are commonly divided into two broad categories: the **print** media (newspapers and magazines) and the **broadcast** media (radio and television). We do not address other forms of media such as books or films here, though much of the information and many of the principles we discuss are transferable to these other media.

In addition to the individual media outlets, several other media organizations and services are important. These are the wire services, syndicates and networks that generate and distribute news and features, and link the individual media outlets together.

What the Media Do

Most of the media can be thought of as trying (each in different proportions) to fulfill four basic functions:

Information: We get most of our information about the outside world from the media. Newspapers and news magazines like *Time* or *Newsweek* focus on recent events; other publications provide more detailed features about a wide range of subjects. Radio and television have news programs too, but they have a heavy entertainment bias. Most people who stay abreast of current affairs rely more on newspapers and magazines than on radio and television for their information.

Influence: The media all have ways in which they openly try to persuade the audience to accept a certain viewpoint. Newspapers and magazines have editorials, opinion pieces and columns. Radio and television have editorials, talk shows and debates. They also influence people subtly, in ways that will be described throughout this book.

Advertising: Advertisements allow a business, individual or organization to draw public attention to their product, service or ideology in exchange for a payment to the publisher or station. By their design or context, advertisements are usually distinguished from the rest of the publication or show where they appear.

Most newspapers and magazines fill over half of their space with advertising, and get the overwhelming majority of their income from it. Except for public broadcasting stations and those that are operated by a church or other group trying to put forth a specific point of view, nearly all broadcast stations get all their income from advertising.

Entertainment: Radio and television hold their audience primarily by providing entertainment. Situation comedies, talk shows, sports, even the news all seek to draw more viewers by being fun to watch or listen to.

The four functions listed above are related, and the relationships are of interest to anyone who is working with the media.

For example, one purpose of entertainment is simple amusement, but this is almost never an end in itself. It is, rather, a means of drawing potential consumers, who will thereby be exposed to advertising, thus increasing the opportunity for the media to collect advertising revenue.

Entertainment is also used for persuasion. Television comedies, cartoons in newspapers, and human-interest stories often carry persuasive messages.

Even more subtle is the power of the media to tell us what subjects are important to think about. In the first half of this century, by almost never mentioning homosexuality, the media strongly conveyed its opinion: homosexuality doesn't exist, or at least it isn't proper to talk about it. The media doesn't always set public policy, but it frequently defines the agenda.

Advertising is, in a sense, another form of persuasion. The goal of advertising is to persuade a potential customer to purchase a product or service, or to accept a specific ideology. And, although it's rare, advertisers have been known to try to influence a media outlet's editorial position.

A more subtle influence of advertising is the reader or viewer profile that the advertiser is seeking. For example, if newspapers were solely supported by sales to readers, then the publisher wouldn't care who the readers were — just how many of them were out there. But advertisers do care; they want to reach people with money to spend, and who are interested in their product, service, or ideology.

Items meant to be purely informative are often subtly — or not so subtly — persuasive. The use of adjectives, the context of an article or story, and the general tone of the delivery can all affect the overall impression the reader or viewer will see or hear.

In short, all of the other functions of the media are related to persuasion.

The Media Organizations

Each of the media goes about its work in its own way. The *New York Times* has different criteria for its selection and presentation of stories than does CBS News; to influence either of them you need to know how those criteria differ.

Newspapers: There are some 1700 daily newspapers and

9000 weeklies in the U.S. While most metropolitan areas once had several competing daily papers, shifting demographics, economics and competition have driven most dailies into consolidations or out of business entirely. Today, many urban areas have only one daily newspaper.

Weeklies are common in smaller towns. They once tended to be locally-owned family enterprises, but the trend today is toward consolidation into newspaper groups or chains. The substance of a weekly is almost entirely local news; it covers events that personally affect readers on a daily basis. Thus, many weeklies are read more carefully and thoroughly than the larger dailies, and may have greater local impact.

Newspapers have five basic divisions. **Editorial** gathers and prepares the news, features, and all other material except advertising. **Advertising** solicits and prepares the display and classified ads. **Production** transforms the editorial and advertising material into type and graphics, and prints the paper. **Circulation** distributes the papers, usually through both newsstands and door-to-door deliveries. **Business** oversees the commercial transactions.

Magazines cover a tremendous range of interests and needs. They can provide information and entertainment in greater depth than can newspapers, but usually in a more specialized field. A few mass-oriented magazines like *Reader's Digest* report in brief on a wide variety of topics. News magazines such as *Time* and *Newsweek* try to cover what the editors perceive as the major news stories of the week. And thousands of specialty magazines give detailed coverage of virtually any subject you can think of, be it coal mining or button collecting or art investments.

Fiction is now mainly the province of mass-market paperback books, and most magazines publish news and non-fiction. Much of their material is produced by freelance writers and photographers, whose work is coordinated by a small editorial staff. Large magazines are more likely to have their own writers, and the newsmagazines sometimes write by committee — a squad of reporters gathers news, another writes it up, another edits it.

The internal structure of magazines is similar to that of newspapers.

Radio and Television: There is no theoretical limit to the number of newspapers and magazines that can exist. Broadcast media, however, rely on the airwaves which would become useless if they got too crowded. For that reason the government — in the U.S., the Federal Communications Commission (FCC) — regulates radio and television broadcasting but does not regulate the distribution of the print media.

In the U.S. there are about 950 television stations and 7800 radio stations. That's about all there was room for in the past; today, with cable TV opening up new transmission methods, we are seeing a dramatic increase in the number of stations.

The FCC requires that broadcasting facilities be licensed on a local basis, and most stations are locally owned. But they are influenced nationally through the networks, which produce some standardized programming and advertising for their local affiliates.

Broadcast Networks: Networks got started in the twenties with the advent of commercial radio, which then faced stiff competition from the newspapers. When fifty local stations each contributed to a single production, they could get back a show that would have been impossible for them to afford individually. For the next three decades, radio dominated home entertainment and the networks dominated radio.

In the fifties, that changed. Television was becoming popular, and radio lost much of its audience. Three major radio networks — CBS, NBC and ABC — moved out of radio and into television. Today radio is more independent than before, but network programming dominates the TV screen; about 60% of all TV programming is centrally controlled.

Wire Services and Syndicates: Wire services and syndicates are wholesalers of news and features. They do not deal directly with the ultimate media consumer — the listening, viewing or reading public — but provide the media outlets, both print and broadcast, with national and international reports, pictures and features beyond the reach of a local media's reporting staff.

Fees are charged to the purchasing media. In the case of wire services, the local clients also must make their own stories available to the other subscribers of the wire service. Because of the huge number of people who are eventually exposed to the information and opinion from the wire services and syndicates, their impact is tremendous.

The two major wire services in the U.S. are the Associated Press (AP) and United Press International (UPI). They have about 2500 clients each, including almost every daily paper, the radio and television networks, local stations, and newsmagazines. Both wire services are based in New York City, with bureaus in almost every large city; in smaller locales their coverage is often handled by part-time correspondents, called **stringers**, who may also be employed by local media. This helps keep costs down, but the use of such a wide range of sources means that the accuracy and consistency may suffer.

UPI executives who were around in 1976 will not need to have this explained to them. That was the year UPI picked up a story from a small Connecticut newspaper about a "horticultural hobbyist" who, in a burst of Bicentennial fever, had developed a new species of pickle — it had red and white stripes on the side with white stars on a blue background at the top. Only trouble was, as the wire services discovered a few hours later, the pickles existed only in the imagination of two soon-unemployed reporters. UPI issued a kill order on the story, and certain faces in the office were as red as — well, as red as a pickle stripe.

This story is true, and funny, but also alarming. If a major wire service lets a story about patriotic pickles get out without checking on it, how can we expect them to catch the more subtle errors and distortions that creep into stories about gay people? We can't — unless we give them some prompting.

While AP and UPI are the two major wire services, some of the major newspapers, like the *New York Times* and the *Los Angeles Times*, are flagships of their own national news services, providing additional news supplements and background information.

In addition to these news services, dozens of feature syndicates provide comics and columns of advice and opinion to their subscribers.

3. Getting Started

So, how do you start talking back? If you picked up this book because you've seen or heard lesbian and gay issues covered by the media in a way that you found offensive, then you've already made a start. In fact, keeping track of what the media are saying and what they are ignoring — in short, *monitoring the media* — is a good first step. It will help you become familiar with the media, as well as providing files of background material that will be useful as you carry out other media projects.

In this chapter, we present some tips we've learned about monitoring the media, and briefly suggest other projects (which we'll explain in more detail in later chapters) that you can do once you've started monitoring.

While you as an individual can carry out many of these projects by yourself, some of them are most effectively (and most enjoyably) executed with other individuals of a media advocacy group. If you're already a member of a gay/lesbian organization, you might form a media committee within that organization, or you might feel it more effective to start a separate group — perhaps a coalition of two or more already existing organizations.

Often the media itself will provide a rallying point around which to start a media advocacy group. When you see or hear something in the media that particularly offends you, chances are it has offended several other people. Assuming the motivational power created by a shared sense of outrage, all you need to start a group is to place notices around the community to announce the time and place for an initial meeting. Be sure to include a phone number where interested people who can't attend the meeting can contact you.

Our group, LAGMA, started in direct response to the poor and inaccurate Boston media coverage of the Lesbian and Gay March on Washington in October, 1979. A few individuals who already knew each other got together to plan a response. A short announcement in Boston's *Gay Community News* brought in several more people, all of whom were outraged by the poor media coverage of the march. Every time the media gives particularly poor or insensitive coverage of lesbian and gay issues, LAGMA's membership increases.

Monitoring the Media

Media monitoring consists of clipping articles from newspapers and magazines, taping or transcribing radio and television programs, keeping a media log and maintaining a file of these clippings, tapes, video recordings and transcriptions.

When you meet with the media, having these examples of what they've done makes it easier to explain why you felt a meeting was necessary. It puts your complaints and suggestions into a real context that makes sense to media representatives. And after such a meeting, it's only by continuing to monitor the media that you can see whether they're living up to any commitments they may have made.

You should try to build a file on each newspaper and TV or radio station that you monitor, showing just what they have and haven't covered, and how. On each newspaper clipping, note the date, publication, page and section where it appeared. The context of the article or story may also be important. (Did the newspaper place its gay pride march coverage on page one, or on the obituary page next to an article headlined "Scout Master Fired After Homosexual Rape"?) When you hear something on the radio or TV, jot down the exact words as closely as you can remember them, the time, the announcer, the station and the program.

This file will be a powerful tool for revealing patterns and attitudes. Soon you'll have a good idea of who your friends are, and who they aren't. When you meet with the media, you'll be doing more than just talking generalities.

If you're doing this by yourself, keeping track of coverage in one daily newspaper or one television station's news coverage may be all you can handle. If you're part of a media group, you can coordinate yourselves to watch much more. Careful study of *T.V. Guide* can alert you to special features that are coming up, but for coverage of news events, there will be no advance notice. If you want to thoroughly cover network programming, and if you have professional-looking stationery for your media group, you may be able to get advance sheets from the networks that summarize the content of upcoming shows.

What the media do say isn't the only important thing. You also need to know what they're ignoring. Subscribe to a gay newspaper that will keep you informed of news events both locally and nationwide in the lesbian and gay community, so you'll know what you might be missing in the mainstream media. In the summer of 1980, for example, the 116,000 Cuban refugees who had recently arrived in Florida were a big story. But the general public never heard about the large number of gay men who were among the refugees until July, when the *Washington Post* ran a major front-page report on them. Readers of at least two gay papers — the *Washington Blade* and the *(San Francisco) Sentinel* — had known about this story right from the start.

Other Projects

Once you've started monitoring the media, you can move on to other projects (some of which we will cover in more depth in later chapters) such as:

• *Writing letters* — including letters to the editor; statements for editorial reply on TV or radio; letters of complaint or praise; letters offering story ideas.

• *Organizing letter-writing or telephone campaigns* — and thus getting the whole community involved in your efforts.

• *Creating news* — suggesting story ideas for news and features; thinking up ways your group or community can attract favorable news coverage. In the Appendix you'll find examples of story ideas that we've given to the media.

• *Arranging meetings with the media* — get-acquainted and follow-up meetings with people in decision-making positions; ongoing meetings to discuss specific concerns or to offer background information; emergency meetings when a specific event creates the possibility of widespread sensational coverage; community ascertainment surveys with broadcasters.

• *Contacting talk shows* — soliciting invitations for speakers from your own and other organizations to appear on TV and radio; offering ideas to producers for interesting gay-related topics.

• *Providing news and background* — calling the news desk to give late-breaking news, or to advise them of upcoming events, and following up with a press release; organizing press conferences when the situation really demands it; providing background information, lists of community contacts, and press kits to the media.

• *Maintaining a press list* — for use by yourselves and other groups when there's something you need to tell the media about.

• *Creating and promoting public service announcements and broadcast editorials* — for radio and TV.

• *And the nitty-gritty of being an organization* — deciding what type of structure to use; getting a mailing address and a professional-looking letterhead printed so that you'll look like a serious group; setting priorities as to which of the above activities to pursue.

4. Analyzing the Media

A program like the CBS "Gay Power, Gay Politics" can mislead millions of straight Americans, but most gay people will quickly see how distorted it is. In other cases the bias can be so subtle that even a well-informed reader will not realize what's going on.

But don't reporters try to be objective?

A reporter's ability to be "objective" is notoriously affected by numerous *subjective* factors, and around the issue of sexual orientation there are few neutral opinions. Subtle influences exist, and a reporter's comfort or discomfort in these areas can greatly affect objectivity.

Imagine that a straight male reporter is interviewing two women candidates for city council, one an open lesbian, the other a married woman. The reporter might feel uncomfortable with the lesbian, subconsciously attributing to her all society's stereotypes about lesbians. He might feel threatened or devalued as a man, and a subtle resentment might thus creep into the writing. Is it any surprise, then, if his article ends up describing the lesbian woman as "rambling" and "aggressive" on an issue while the married woman is noted to be "eloquent" and "devoted" to a cause? Bias? No doubt. Can you prove it? Not without a lot more evidence — and a probe of the subconscious.

Ah, but what if that same reporter were a gay man or a

lesbian? Don't be so sure that would change anything. Chances are he or she is very much in the closet at work, and is thinking, "Better be careful. If I make her sound too good the editor might wonder why."

Even if a reporter doesn't have strong feelings about a story, the newspaper's publisher or editor might. One journalism professor decided to test this influence in his journalism class. He gave students a story topic, and told half the class that story was being written for a liberal newspaper, half that it was for a conservative paper. With no further instructions than that, most students slanted the story so as to reflect the policy of the newspaper; students who disagreed with the policy actually slanted the story to *more* strongly reflect the policy of the paper!

And, of course, some reporters won't even try to be objective. Recently, when a gay activist in Boston was on trial he saw a reporter talking to the District Attorney. He went over and asked if the reporter would listen to his side of the story too. "I'm not talking to any homos," the reporter said and walked away.

How else does media bias show up?

Between the time that a reporter gathers information about a story, and the time that it appears in print or on the air, a lot of people handle it. There are a number of ways that bias can creep in, some of which are discussed below.

The homosexual adjective: "Homosexual murders are frequent, and sadomasochistic practices... relatively frequent in homosexuality," reports *Time*. Homosexual murder, homosexual torture, homosexual rape, even, we are told, gay arson. And yet, can you *ever* recall seeing the terms heterosexual rape, heterosexual child abuse, heterosexual wife-battering? Probably not, though heterosexual rapes clearly outnumber same-sex rapes and lurid stories of wife and child dismemberment fill the weekly tabloids.

Years ago, many newspapers would identify a criminal suspect as black if that were the case, but said nothing about race when a suspect was white. Most of them have stopped doing that, but the same bias still exists around the labeling of a person's sexual orientation when a crime is involved. If John Hinckley had declared that he tried to assassinate Ronald Reagan in order to demonstrate his love for Robert DeNiro instead of for Jodie Foster, his *homosexuality* would have been a major news angle to the story. As it is, no one refers to his *heterosexuality*. In other words, as in reporting racial characteristics, the press should either omit the homosexual/heterosexual adjective altogether, or else *routinely* use it in all cases — at which point most readers would be shocked to see how numerous are "heterosexual" crimes.

Placement: The story about a lesbian and gay pride march of 10,000 people can get a front-page story, or it can get a one-paragraph notice buried inside. Where it ends up tells a lot about how important the news editor thinks that march was. Similarly, if the coverage of such a march is put on the same page as an exposé on a senator found soliciting sex in the men's room, the public's view that *anything* connected with the word homosexual is either sexual or sordid, is again reinforced.

Stereotypes: How the march gets reported is also revealing. Do the media give a realistic overview of the march, or do the cameras zoom in only on those who *confirm* existing stereotypes and on the most flamboyant?

Background: Does the reporter know enough background to report on the significance of a story? Many of the marchers are risking their jobs, their friends, even their family ties by publicly identifying themselves as gay. Do the media discuss this, or is the march reported as simply one more parade, a sort of lavender St. Patrick's Day celebration?

Isolation: It's important for the media to cover that march, and other specifically gay events, but it's also important for them not to isolate us, not to present us as something separate from the rest of the world. When your local newspaper does a feature on teenage sexuality, do they mention the problems facing gay youth, and the resources available to them? When there's a television special about "The Church in a Changing World," does it mention the impact of gay religious organizations like Dignity or Integrity? And little things: we need to see more comments like this one, from a *Boston Globe* review of the film *Conan*: "Might makes right, [the film] says, and violence is okay as long as it gets you power. Men are Nietzchean supermen, heterosexual killing machines (one ugly scene mocks homosexuals) constantly at war...." Such reporting is a rarity; we need to see more reporters who can bring a consciousness of homophobia into other writing.

Lesbian invisibility: While gay men have always been fair game for excessive stigmatization, and the details of their sex lives often the focus of sensationalistic reporting, lesbians have been virtually ignored. Both the terms "homosexual" and "gay" often connote males only.

In part, this is clearly a *feminist* issue: reporters defer to males, ask men their opinions, focus on gay male activists. Since lesbians are women and "women's issues" are lower on the priority list, lesbians and their opinions rarely appear in the media. Perhaps too, lesbians are seen as too threatening, and not as much "fun" as heterosexual women for male reporters to interview.

There is one exception. Apparently the sensationalism attached to lesbian mother custody cases is sufficient to warrant their coverage. Thus, the personal anguish of these women, as they attempt to convince often-prejudiced judges of their adequacy as mothers, has become public domain.

The laundry list of social evils: "... an area populated with derelicts, homosexuals and drug addicts" says the paper, and once more the reader's stereotypes and erroneous associations are subconsciously strengthened. The phone at that newspaper should be ringing with so many complaints that they think twice before being so off-handed with us in the future.

Photographs: Pictures taken at night, or that are grainy or of poor quality, can distort the meaning of an accompanying article, especially when the words say one thing but the images, another.

Hitler's opinion: A nazi would not be required in a discussion of anti-Semitism, nor would a member of the Ku Klux Klan be called in for a discussion of civil rights for black Americans. However, it is *common* for members of the clergy, the psychiatric profession, and right-wing groups such as the Moral Majority who hold clear anti-gay opinions to be included in discussions of the civil rights of gays and lesbians.

Sensationalism: When a recent fire destroyed $6 million worth of property in San Francisco, the fire chief told reporters that, based on a tip, he feared gay men had burned to death chained to beds in "slave quarters." The media couldn't have asked for a better way to sell newspapers, and the story made headlines everywhere. When the truth surfaced it was less exciting — no one was killed in the fire, and there were no slave quarters — and it got far less media play. For the general public, the image of gay men chained to their beds, burning to death from a fire caused by their own recklessness, will persist long after the physical ashes of the fire are cleaned up.

Similarly, the incessant emphasis on "sex" in homosexual, when we actually engage in a multitude of activities besides sex, is a sensationalistic distortion of the richness and complexity of our *total* lives.

Vocabulary: There are tens of thousands of words in the English language. A reporter can, perhaps subconsciously, find one that is technically accurate for a situation but that influences the reader in whatever direction the reporter wishes. Thus, a gay bar may be described as "crowded" whereas if it were straight, it would be "popular". Someone can be called an "admitted homosexual" or "avowed lesbian" and it sounds pretty awful; much worse, certainly, that being "openly gay".

Who gets quoted? Many reporters will try to seem objective by attributing to someone else every debatable statement in a story. Thus even if the statement is false, the story is technically accurate because the quote is accurate. A story about a demonstration, for example, might quote police and official sources a dozen times, the protesters once or perhaps not at all.

This is bad enough when the parties quoted are trying to be truthful; it's worse when they're not. The *Boston Globe*, in a story about two men arrested for allegedly having sex with a minor, made nine statements about what supposedly happened. Six of them were attributed to a Detective Ulrich or other police sources; three were simply stated as unattributed facts. The men arrested were not quoted at all. "Ulrich said... [that police] seized what amounted to 'child pornography,'" says the story. The police didn't seize child pornography at all, but what reader is going to doubt the story? For that matter, the *Globe*'s own headline writer was mislead by the story; the headline for this story incorrectly said "Two men arrested in Dorchester as 'child pornography' suspects". The paper eventually printed a correction but, like most corrections, it could not possibly undo the harm that had been done to these two men.

Just the facts: The *Globe* story is just one example of how the media, without technically straying from the facts, can nonetheless distort reality. In any news story there will be more facts than can fit into the space available; a responsible reporter will look at all the information available, and use those facts that give the best possible picture of reality.

Terms of blatant abuse: Epithets such as "queer", "lezzie" and the like are rarely encountered these days except in the extremely conservative press or straight men's porn, but plays on words like "fruit" or "dyke" and other malicious attempts at humor are still used by columnists, and on talk and game shows. This is as unacceptable as racial and ethnic slurs.

Gresham's Law of Public Relations: "Bad images drive out good," writes Randy Alfred in *The Advocate*. "If the gay angle is essentially irrelevant to the story's news value, it will be mentioned only if the story is negative. An alleged arsonist who claims to be gay is a 'gay arsonist,' but a humanitarian doctor who's partly closeted is a 'bachelor.'"

What else needs to be considered in analyzing media coverage?

First, look at the source of the story. When a newspaper runs a biased story from AP or UPI, that may just indicate sloppy or insensitive editing. If a staff reporter had written the story, it would be evidence of a different sort of problem.

Also, differentiate between the various types of stories. Coverage of spontaneous news that is just breaking — an arrest, an accident, a murder — is always under deadline pressures and errors are common. During the assassination attempt on President Reagan in 1981, the media were at first reporting that press secretary Brady had been killed. If a mistake like that can happen on a major story with dozens of reporters around, imagine how much more likely mistakes are when just one highly-pressured reporter is involved.

News stories that can be anticipated — a press conference, a trial, or a demonstration, for example — should receive somewhat more accurate coverage.

Feature stories, because they aren't rushed into print under deadline pressures, should be the most accurate of all

— if the writer wants them that way. If they're not, it's time for you to respond.

A lot of guidelines have been given here for analyzing a story. But it's not as complicated as it sounds. Ultimately, you should just ask how you feel after reading a story: Are you angry? Do you feel put down? Trivialized? If your parents read this story, would it heighten their understanding, or would it contribute to their misunderstanding, of you as a lesbian or gay man? In the final analysis, many times it is the subtlety of feeling conveyed in a story that most influences the public.

5. Response

It's Sunday morning. You get the morning paper and sit down to relax with a fresh cup of hot coffee. Then you read the headline: "Forty die in homosexual fire", and promptly drop your coffee on the floor. Now what do you do?

Well, first you clean up the coffee. As for doing something about that headline, you have more options than you might think, ranging from a simple phone call to an organized demonstration.

Is a phone call really that effective?

Yes. It's probably even more effective than we know, and if you're not going to get around to doing anything else, a phone call is certainly easy and far more effective than doing nothing. Recently a LAGMA member saw an especially good news report on Boston's 1982 Lesbian and Gay Pride March. She promptly picked up the phone to register her praise. The person at the other end was *very* appreciative, and said that this was the first positive call they'd gotten; numerous people had called in to complain. Clearly these immediate phone responses were having an impact.

Try to phone in the daytime, when the responsible editor is likely to be around. Explain just what happened, and why you found it objectionable. You probably won't be able to reach the reporter who covered the story, nor is he or she necessarily the person you should be talking to; an editor will have more influence in getting a correction, if that's appropriate, or preventing a recurrence of the problem.

Who is this "responsible editor"?

With a newspaper or magazine, note the section — main news section, sports pages, lifestyle, local news or whatever — where the article appeared. Ask on the phone or check the masthead to find out who the editor for that section is; that person is the responsible editor.

With broadcast media, call the station to find out who produces the show in question.

How can I make them take my complaint seriously?

Promptness is important; register your complaint within 24 hours. If you wait a week they'll have forgotten about the story. Besides, they'll figure if it took you a week to complain, you probably weren't all that bothered by it anyway.

Second, be accurate. With a newspaper story, make a note on your clipping of the date, paper, section of the paper and even which edition it appeared in. With radio and television it's harder to get an exact record of what was said, but as soon as you hear something offensive, write it down, along with the relevant data about who said it, when, on what program and what station.

Before you phone with your complaint, try to briefly put into words exactly why it was objectionable. You'll be most effective if you speak to someone in a position of authority and can quickly, courteously make them understand that, by their own professional standards, they blew it. Then follow up with a letter.

What should I try to say in a letter?

That depends on whether or not it's a "letter to the editor" meant for publication. Whenever you phone in a complaint, it will help if you can follow up with a not-for-publication letter.

This letter should follow some of the same guidelines as the phone call. Address it to a person with some degree of editorial authority; give the details of when and where the offending story appeared; write it as soon as possible; and be as brief and as courteous as your grievance and your patience allow.

Letters have more impact than phone calls, and you should use them both for maximum effect. You can also make several copies of a letter; address the main letter to the appropriate editor, and send copies to the reporter who covered the story, the managing editor, the publisher, and anyone else who seems relevant. With no additional writing, and for the cost of a few extra stamps, you'll increase your effectiveness considerably.

Are these letters really effective?

Yes. In many cases, your letter will be the only one generated by a particular story; in all but the most controversial cases, your letter will be one of a mere handful responding to it.

In the case of broadcast media, you can also write to the companies that sponsor offensive programs. In the late 1970s, a group called the National Citizens Committee for Broadcasting began a campaign against the heavy emphasis on violence on TV. It organized a study to determine which were the most violent programs, and it published a list of the advertisers that were supporting those shows. Kodak was one of the companies named.

"We were quite shocked to be on the NCCB list," said a Kodak representative. "We got a few hundred letters. The company felt strongly that it did not want to be visible on that list or any such list," and asked its ad agency to stop placing Kodak ads on the more violent shows. Other companies did the same.

Compared with the hundreds of millions of people who watch network TV, the few hundred who wrote letters were statistically insignificant. Yet they influenced the ad policies of many multinational corporations. Likewise a dozen people in your community, who send in a complaint each time they see or hear something homophobic in the media and who send some praise each time they see good coverage, can have quite an impact.

We cannot overemphasize the importance of this letter-writing. Widespread public apathy results in very few people taking the time to respond in writing to what they see or hear in the media. Those who do respond most vehemently are often those who are against us; thus it becomes even more important to make sure we at least balance their responses with our own.

What about letters that are meant for publication?

Two of the same principles are especially important in that case: respond promptly, and be brief.

A good letter can do one of several things:
• Point out how an article has biased or distorted reality, perhaps through some of the techniques in the last chapter;
• Correct inaccuracies, or add important information that was missing from a story;
• Draw attention to a story that was omitted or trivialized;
• Praise or criticize an editorial or columnist's comment on lesbian or gay issues. Praise is every bit as important as criticism.

Letters to the editor in newspapers and magazines are especially important because they are a way both to give feedback to those determining policy, and if they are printed, they will have some influence on public opinion — *if* the invisible hand of the editor is fair in the selection and editing of the letters. But of course, editors aren't always fair. Study the letters page over a period of time. Are homophobic letters common? Do intelligent letters from lesbians and gay men appear?

How can I do all that in one letter?

You usually can't. So choose one or two points that you want to make, and concentrate on expressing them well.

A long letter will almost never be published without

considerable editing — editing over which you have no control, and which can make mush out of the brilliant argument that you developed at such length. Better that you should edit it yourself, before the letter is ever mailed.

What if my letters never get printed?

Keep a copy of your letters, and ask others to do the same; your media advocacy group can keep a file of these copies. Armed with them, you'll have a strong case when you meet with the editor to discuss *why* the opinions in these letters aren't getting into print.

Meanwhile, don't think your letters are having no effect at all. By writing frequently, you're alerting the publication to the existence of a concerned and critical gay audience. In fact, public response in the form of letters and phone calls are important to any publication as a way of gauging how well it's doing its job. One of the first goals of a media advocacy group should be to encourage everyone they know — individuals, members of other gay and lesbian groups, even straight friends and relatives — to do more letter-writing.

Some people will be reluctant to sign their name to a letter that might appear in print. This can be turned to advantage by explaining in the letter that "I would like to sign my name but I could stand to lose my job if I did so," and signing off with "Name Withheld on Request." (Most newspapers or magazines will still want to know the writer's name. If that's still unacceptable, the anonymous writer will have to find someone else to sign the letter.)

What about form letters and petitions?

You may be tempted to compose and print a form letter, which your friends and supporters need only sign and mail. This will certainly insure that a lot of letters are sent with minimal effort — but the media will realize that too, and such letters or petitions get little attention. Your efforts are better spent assisting your allies in writing their own individual letters. Remember: you want these letters to represent a broad base of community support, not the results of a well-oiled machine.

How do I handle a subject that just can't be adequately covered in a short letter?
You could try a longer letter. Where there is a clear need for such length, some publications will occasionally print a longer piece.

Many papers also provide op-ed forums. These exist specifically for individuals and groups that need more space to comment on a significant issue than a letter allows. Be alert, though, to the possibility of hostile editing of your writing; if the suggested editing interferes with what you're trying to say, you may wish to pull the piece entirely or talk to the periodical about their standards.

Make a note of any other forums that your paper offers for readers to express their views. There could be a "Chatters" page, a forum for the exchange of practical tips and advice, in what may yet be called the Women's Section. In many papers this has expanded far beyond a sharing of recipes and patterns; often it contains the personal comments of women on such vital issues as wife-battering, alcoholism, drug-use by teenagers, and so on. Why not, then, have a note from a lesbian mother asking for advice on how to come out to her children, or from a parent of a lesbian, or from an older woman who has come out? If we start feeling free to share our lives in these sections, we will be helping to demystify and normalize "homosexuality" as well as providing support for millions of closeted people out there.

If these contributions are never published, then it's time to approach the editors for a meeting. But our feeling is that most often such letters would be printed *if we wrote them*. The problem is, we must first raise our own expectations enough that we'll submit such material.

There may also be a locally-based advice columnist, to whom you could address the questions and issues that concern you. Syndicated columnists like "Dear Abby" and "Ann Landers" reach millions of readers and your letter to them is unlikely to appear in print — but it can help to educate them, or to support them if they've taken a positive stand on a gay issue.

Recent years have seen a noticeable shift in the attitudes of the more prominent national advice columnists on the subject of homosexuality. In a TV interview in June of 1982, Ann Landers acknowledged that numerous letters over the years from happy, healthy lesbians and gay men, as well as the latest scientific research, have changed her position on this issue.

What about responding to radio and television broadcasts?

Radio and TV can't print letters to the editor, but otherwise the same principles apply to them as to the print media: Go to the right person, do it promptly, be accurate about what happened, when, and where, and state your grievance — or praise — as succinctly as you can.

With the broadcast media, you have further advantages because of the Federal Communications Commission. Broadcasters must keep letters that they receive, in special files for review when their license comes up for renewal; these files are also open to the public. This does not apply to the major networks themselves, since they don't hold broadcast licenses, but it does apply to stations they own, to their affiliates, and to local independent stations.

Under the current trend toward government deregulation of the media, areas such as broadcast station licensing and application of the fairness doctrine may change. Check with the FCC for up-to-date information. It has offices in many large cities; the address for its main headquarters is in the Appendix.

Most television and some radio stations have a public affairs or community relations staff to handle the multiple and sometimes conflicting demands of their several constituencies. They are not policy-makers but buffers between the outside world and management. Occasionally they'll have real influence, but not often. Don't allow yourself to be shunted off to them unless it's clear that they can really do something.

How can I get my opinion voiced on the air?

Talk shows, especially live radio shows, frequently encourage their home audience to call in. Do so if you can be articulate under fire. It may help to prepare notes to refer to while talking. Remember that most listeners know very little about gay issues. You don't need to come up with any amazing new insights; the ideas and arguments that you've heard a hundred times will be a revelation to others.

The FCC also requires broadcasters to provide air time for conflicting viewpoints. Under its fairness doctrine, a broadcast station is obliged to present both sides of a "controversial issue of public importance." If a fundamentalist preacher speaks out against gay civil rights legislation, the station must make time for proponents of the bill. There are some catches, though. They have to cover the pro–gay rights viewpoint but they don't necessarily have to give it *equal* time. The FCC has ruled that even if one view gets five times as much coverage as the other, that is still an acceptable balance of views. Another FCC regulation assures that groups or individuals who are mentioned *by name* are entitled to reply if an attack has been made on their honesty, character or integrity. In such cases the station must provide the person or group with a transcript of what was said in the event of an appeal to the FCC. Statements made in the context of news coverage are exempt from this provision.

In 1981, a *T.V. Guide* article about the fairness doctrine described a case that illustrates this. A gay rights activist had heard an extremely anti-gay sermon on TV, and complained to the local station. The station ultimately reduced the airtime for that show. Letters to the editor that appeared subsequently in *T.V. Guide* praised the magazine for its coverage of this sensitive, controversial issue.

Stations may also voluntarily provide an individual or a group with air time on an editorial or other programming done by that station. Usually this is a brief time, perhaps just one minute, during which you or a staff announcer can read a prepared statement. The station will want to read over the copy before it is aired.

When are complaints not appropriate?

Before you complain, be sure there is really distorted or discriminatory reporting going on. You *can't* complain when the newspaper runs a story about a psychopath who sexually assaults and kills several males. You *can* complain if it refers to these as "homosexual killings" but never uses the phrase "heterosexual killings." A good way to get written off as a paranoid nut is to start making unwarranted complaints.

What about praise?

It is *vital* that we praise good coverage as well as criticize the bad; it frequently takes courage for those working in the media to oppose the peer pressure of homophobia that exists in these straight-dominated environments. *Never* take a supportive attitude in the media for granted. It is all too rare, and needs to be encouraged with a kind word at the right time. Positive reinforcement will impress upon the media the audience's desire to see more and better.

It is all too easy to skip this aspect of media advocacy; often a program or article that portrays us in a positive light will draw only condemnatory letters, and thus, in the case of newspapers, only those letters will be printed. In 1981, on the front page of its Living section, the *Boston Globe* ran an article about a lesbian grandmother. It was a story that would delight any lesbian or gay activist: a sensitive, humane story about the courage of a woman who came out at the age of 72.

Unfortunately, the *Globe* received numerous letters complaining about this "distasteful" subject and apparently got few letters of appreciation. One of these negative letters appeared as a Letter to the Editor. It was full of prejudice and innuendo, with remarks about "grandma Sappho" and "leering lesbians" in bars. Since the editors try to print letters that represent the response they've received, the publication of this letter indicates that they got far more criticism than praise for the article.

Thus, letters of praise become as important as letters of outrage. In the absence of *our* response, an editor can only conclude that the negative response represents what the public wants. Reports trying to give better coverage of our lives will have a hard time convincing their editor to allow another positive piece.

When writing a letter of praise, always point out exactly what you liked in the article or coverage, and why you liked it. If there was still a problem of some sort, say so cautiously. You want to cultivate an ally, not split hairs. Coming out in favor of gay and lesbian civil rights is as much a gradual process as coming out of the closet itself.

6. Meeting with the Media

Probably the most effective media activity, for the energy it requires, is to meet with media representatives personally to discuss your concerns. What we say here applies to meetings with local newspapers; a meeting with a radio or television station will not be too different.

First you'll have to convince the editor that such a meeting is a good idea. Send a letter — preferably on your group's letterhead — explaining why a meeting with your group could help them provide better and more accurate coverage. If there have been specific problems recently, refer to them as examples of your concern, but emphasize that you want to concentrate on the present and the future. Make it clear that you have no desire to be censors or to impose your news judgment on theirs, but merely want to offer yourselves as a resource, to discuss possible story ideas and to point out some considerations they may not have thought about when reporting on the gay and lesbian community.

A few days after they've received the letter, telephone to see if they're willing to meet and to arrange the details. You'll have to be flexible about time and dates — remember, they have deadlines to work around — but don't compromise about the people with whom you want to meet. Insist that policy-makers be included. If you're passed off onto the community-relations staff, the editors aren't taking you seriously.

Preparing for the meeting

Once the meeting is arranged, you've got some homework to do. Start by finding out just what kind of coverage the paper has provided in the past. If someone has been monitoring it, they can provide this information; otherwise a trip to the library is in order. Make copies of the articles that best dramatize the points you'll want to make, both good and bad.

Then plan your strategy. What will your agenda be? What are the main points you want to make, and who will make them? What are your major objectives? Only if everyone has agreed in advance on your goals can you be sure discussion does not get sidetracked.

Who will be there?

Five or six people from your group, preferably a mixture of men and women, is a reasonable maximum. More than that can easily get chaotic.

Assuming you've gotten through to policy-makers at the newspaper, you'll be meeting with several of the following people:

• *The Publisher* represents, or is, the paper's owner. Usually the publisher leaves the day-to-day operation of the paper to editors, and is not likely to be represented at a meeting like this except in the case of smaller newspapers.

• *The Managing Editor*, sometimes known as the editor-in-chief or executive editor, coordinates all operations.

• *The City Editor* directs local reporters, maintains channels to government, business, colleges, sports and other large institutions, and reviews stories as they come in.

• *National and Foreign Editors* do the same with correspondents covering national and international stories.

• *Department Editors.* Most newspapers have at least a sports department and a culture/entertainment department. The larger the paper, the greater the number of such departments and sections: business, finance, lifestyle, and so on. The editors make assignments and oversee the coverage, and are responsible to either the Managing or City Editor.

• *The Editorial Page Editor* selects and edits letters, chooses political cartoons, and works with the columnists and other contributors to these op/ed pages. This editor usually answers directly to the publisher and is not subordinate to the news department.

The Agenda

A meeting like this can't follow any rigid agenda, but you should have a clear idea beforehand about what you want to accomplish. Those goals may include:

1. A presentation by your group of why you think past coverage has sometimes been distorted or inadequate. The strength of this presentation will establish that you are to be taken seriously, but you must *not* be hostile in your approach if you want to get anything else accomplished. You're trying to work with the media toward the goal of improved coverage.

2. Suggestions on how coverage could be improved.

3. Explanations by the editors of how they operate, and an opportunity for them to ask you questions.

4. A discussion of their employment policy regarding sexual orientation.

5. Encouragement for more and stronger editorial support of gay civil rights legislation.

6. Presenting story ideas, and a list of people and groups that they can call about gay and lesbian issues.

7. Changing or adding to their style handbook.

The Meeting

That could be your written agenda. But in dealing with the issue of sexual orientation, you'll also discover an unwritten agenda of the unspoken questions that will be on everyone's mind.

For example, how comfortable do the editors and reporters feel sitting in a roomful of "homosexuals"? What are their unarticulated preconceptions? Do they personally know anyone who is openly gay or lesbian?

In LAGMA, we've come to expect to have to do a certain amount of consciousness-raising at our meetings with the media, and certainly this *unwritten* agenda can become the key in changing personal attitudes and thus in affecting subsequent coverage. At some point in our meeting we often ask what questions they have; and we'll hear "Why do you use the word 'gay'?" or "How do homosexuals really face discrimination?" The Appendix lists some of the most commonly asked questions.

So, we take a deep breath and start. We share *personal* pain, we talk of our families, we relate incidents. We strive to meet media people *where they are* and slowly raise their consciousness on the issues. We know we are serving as role models for them. By the time we're through they know we have mothers and fathers, they know we often drop our lovers' hands in public, they know that our beloveds' names are often omitted in obituaries.

What does this have to do with our written agenda? Everything. Precisely because we respect the subtle ways that attitudes are influenced, we know that anything that can change these attitudes will ultimately affect what gets printed.

We will also point out that these meetings are often very painful personally. As with other minorities who feel assaulted by the majority's misunderstanding of their lives, we often feel emotionally debilitated by such meetings. But they have *always* raised the awareness of the participants, and we have *always* made at least one personal contact.

Therefore, keeping in mind this unwritten agenda and the fact that some of the editors or reporters you're meeting with are likely to be uncomfortable about the meeting, do your best to make it friendly or at least business-like. You may hear comments that appall you or that show utter ignorance. Update or correct them as appropriate, but don't attack.

The reason for the meeting, after all, is that you may have insights and perceptions they lack. The satisfaction you might get from winning an argument in a closed room is nothing compared to the good that could come from a feature story on local resources available to gay teenagers. Anyone who *doesn't* feel they can keep their temper under control at such a meeting shouldn't attend it. Use members of your group who work well together, who can get each other *out* of tight spots and arguments. Use your most eloquent members.

To discuss how coverage could be improved, go down the list we give in chapter four of how stories are often distorted. Most of the points there will suggest an obvious antidote: reporters should interview lesbians as well as gay men when covering a story that affects both; "homosexual" is inappropriate as an adjective for "murder" or "torture"; and so on. Sometimes it will be useful to make the analogy with treatment of other minorities: if stories about them aren't treated sensationally, then neither should stories about gays.

As this book is being written, the *San Francisco Chronicle* is the only daily newspaper in the U.S. that has actively sought to hire a gay reporter. Few papers have even one openly gay person in their editorial department. You're not likely to convince your local daily to specifically seek out a gay man or lesbian the next time they're hiring a reporter — though it might be worth a try. You *do* have a chance of convincing them that coverage of the lesbian and gay community will be much better if there's someone on the staff who can be approached by reporters and editors who are unsure how to handle a story with a gay theme. That means, for starters, a non-discrimination clause in the employment policy. It also means creating an environment where gay people will feel comfortable about coming out: no more fag jokes in the news room.

The March-April 1982 *Columbia Journalism Review* ran a cover story about media coverage of gay news; it included an interview with Joe Nicholson, a reporter who came out while he was working at the *New York Post*. "Coming out changed my relationships with fellow reporters in unexpected ways," said Nicholson. He became the in-house expert on gay affairs, and greatly helped other reporters who wanted to be sensitive to gay concerns but didn't always know how to handle that angle in a story. "One reporter asked about the "theory" that homosexuals have a propensity to commit arson — one myth that I confessed was new to me. Another showed me a story he had written on a robbery trio that specialized in subway-john holdups, mostly of homosexuals, and asked if it would offend gay people. I said I thought it would serve as a healthy warning to would-be victims as well as a prod to the transit cops to catch the bandits."

Randy Shilts, who was hired by the *San Francisco Chronicle* as an openly gay reporter, had similar experiences. "I think a lot of dumb things that are written because of ignorance, not malice, don't appear because [colleagues] can come to me and feel like they're getting things in clear perspective."

If someone at the meeting seems to be gay

One or more gay men or lesbians may attend the meeting as representatives of the paper. Our experience has been that lesbians and gays in the media do *not* feel safe, for some of the same reasons that the meeting was set up. They do not want to be singled out by us in any way; in fact, merely attending the meeting can be threatening for them. We can, however, try to be supportive of them. We do this each time we ask whether, if the paper has lesbian and gay reporters, those reporters would feel free to make this known. Just by our presence we can serve as positive role models for the most closeted reporters.

Give them your suggestions

Newspapers find the bad news on their own. They may need help finding the good news, and to have potential feature material pointed out to them. But if you've made a good case for yourselves, they should be open to your suggestions for positive news and feature stories. Make up a list of your ideas, with names of contact people, and give a copy to each person at the meeting. It might include:

• The doctor who volunteers time to organize a health clinic serving the needs of the gay community; or of other people doing similar community service work;

• A feature about the problems facing gay youth, or older gays, or lesbian mothers, or gay teachers, in your community, and the resources available to them;

• A story about the Stonewall riots, on an anniversary of the event; and other educational articles to enlighten people who have no knowledge of the gay and lesbian community;

• Profiles of local gay organizations: a hotline, religious organization, or community center.

You can also give out copies of written guidelines for handling gay issues, such as the National Gay Task Force's "Media Guide to Gay Issues," LAGMA's style suggestions, a list of story ideas, or material your advocacy group has prepared; see Appendix for sample style and story ideas.

Help them establish contacts in your community

Give everyone an annotated list of names, addresses and phone numbers for both individuals and organizations in the lesbian and gay community who they can call with questions, for comment both on- and off-the-record, or just to get background for a story in progress.

The wire services

Information from the wire services in most large urban areas is not cycled through the New York headquarters en route to other terminals. What is submitted by editors in Chicago comes out printed verbatim in Portland. So the work you do with your local newspaper will also help to improve the wire service coverage. There are two other steps you can take in this area.

First, ensure that the papers and stations you meet with will edit all releases before they are used. That a story came in over the wire does not mean it needn't maintain the same standards as if it were written by a staff reporter — standards that will hopefully be getting higher as you meet with the media.

Second, meet with the staff of the local wire service bureau. They employ reporters and editors independently, and probably need the same consciousness-raising as a newspaper does.

The broadcast media

The print media have no obligation to talk to anybody about how well they're doing their job, though usually they'll make some effort to be obliging. TV broadcasters *are* required to meet with community members.

These meetings chiefly take the form of a *community ascertainment survey*. Each calendar year, all television stations (with a few unimportant exceptions) are required to interview community leaders representing nineteen concerns in the city of license. These elements run the gamut from Agriculture to Religion.

In March of 1980 the Federal Communications Commission rejected a proposal that they add the specific category of gay people to this list. Instead, they modified the category "other" to ensure that *all* significant elements in the particular community are included in the ascertainment. You can make a strong case that this includes the lesbian and gay community.

Ascertainment is a continuous process; there is no deadline you must meet and community leaders may step forward at any time. But who is a community leader? Are you yourself, or the people in your group, qualified to represent the lesbian and gay population of your area? Unless your group is structured as a coalition, you may want to contact the other organizations in your local gay community so that they'll also be involved in defining your needs.

Until recently, radio stations were also required to hold these ascertainment surveys. Under the recent trend toward deregulation that obligation has been dropped.

Your ascertainment will have most of the same goals, and will require much of the same preparation, as a meeting with a newspaper. But several things will be different. First, because they have these meetings so often, with so many groups, the station may treat the whole thing more routinely than does the newspaper. They have a lot of practice in seeming interested in what you have to say, while not letting you take up too much of their time. Second, if you don't have actual transcripts of comments or reporting that you found objectionable, you'll have to rely more on your ability to do general consciousness-raising.

The names, addresses and organizational affiliations of the people surveyed, plus the information collected in these ascertainments, will be placed in the station's Public Inspection File (PIF) — records that are examined by the FCC when the station's license comes up for renewal. From the file, a list of the most important problems in the community will be drawn and ranked numerically. The top ten are the ones most likely to be given attention.

The Public Inspection File of each station is open to you. Theoretically you could simply walk in and ask to see it without advance notice, but the simple courtesy of calling in advance will probably get more cooperation in the long run. Inspecting this file before a meeting can be a lot of work, but will reveal just what kind of response a station has received to its gay-related coverage.

IF THE MEDIA WON'T MEET WITH YOU....

If a newspaper or broadcast station has been continually abusive to gay men and lesbians, and letters, phone calls and requests for meetings have gotten you nowhere, don't give up. You have other options.

Complain to the FCC

The current trend is for the Federal Communications Commission to do less regulation of the broadcast media than previously — and it has no jurisdiction at all over the print media. Still, if a station is consistently giving distorted and unfair coverage, a complaint to the FCC can be very threatening.

Appeal to media and professional associations

Most professions in the U.S. have some mechanism for monitoring themselves, if for no other reason than to maintain their overall reputation. These watchdog groups rarely have any official power, but they may carry a great deal of influence.

In 1973, the National News Council was created in the U.S. Its goal: to investigate charges of media bias in national news coverage and to release its findings. It was this Council that found CBS guilty of distortion in its "Gay Power, Gay Politics" documentary.

Several journalism reviews around the country report on how well the press is doing its job. The *Columbia Journalism Review* is the most prominent of these; a dishonorable mention in its DARTS AND LAURELS column can cause considerable embarrassment.

Demonstrations

If nothing else works, a demonstration may get a media organization to take your complaints seriously. First, however, you'll need to think it through carefully. Will this step embarrass the media into reconsidering its position, or will it simply make them feel like getting back at you?

The demonstration itself may be staged as a media event. The more creative the idea you have for your protest, the easier this will be. Other media (especially those in direct competition with the target of your protest) should be contacted with the news that something unusual is about to happen down at the *Daily Planet* building. When they show up, spokespersons from your group should be prepared to articulate your grievances and to pass out a printed press release about the event.

If you announce a demonstration and only three members of your group show up, you'll look pretty silly. Before you do something of this sort, be sure that some of the people involved in the planning have organized demonstrations before, and that you can get enough of a turnout to avoid embarrassing yourselves.

7. Continuing Media Work

Your initial meeting with a newspaper or broadcast station should have had some influence on the people you met; it may even have resulted in some official policy changes. But you've still got a long way to go. There are lots more people in the organization who you didn't meet, and new ones are coming in all the time. Even the people you did meet with may regress if you don't keep up pressure on them.

The *you* in all this doesn't have to be a gay media group specifically. It can be any gay group or individual with the persistence to keep working in this field. By virtue of your having approached them calmly and knowledgeably, the media are going to think of you as community leaders. Fine, but you'll be even more effective if others know how to approach the media independently, to express their own concerns. And the more, the better. We recommend that you — whoever that consists of — share your growing expertise with the rest of the community.

How a newspaper functions

Editors and reporters adhere to tight deadlines, and are constantly planning ahead. All news media have contingency plans to account for major, unexpected news such as assassinations or earthquakes. With all the unpredictable variables in the news, order and routine are essential if work is to get done on time.

Morning newspapers are composed by night, after most

news-producing events in that time zone or locality have occurred, and are more stable and predictable than afternoon papers, which are put together while the news is happening. Afternoon papers outnumber morning papers in the U.S. by about four to one.

The newspaper cycle begins with the editors' review of scheduled news events, such as meetings and press conferences, spontaneous news that may have happened overnight, and news that is still developing. The editors evaluate news possibilities, decide on priorities for coverage, and assign reporters.

Throughout the day, reporters keep in touch with their editors, who revise their priorities and plan accordingly. By afternoon the reporters return to write their stories. In the case of late-breaking stories, the reporters may phone in their information to rewriters, who compose articles and headlines on the spot. The editors choose which among the many stories will be printed, and send them along to copy editors for editing and headlines. The completed stories then go to the composing rooms to be typeset, and finally to the press room for printing.

A large newspaper will use only a small percentage of the stories it receives; the rest are either thrown away, filed for a limited time, or submitted to the wire services, because there simply is not room for all of them. The various people who select which stories are to be seen are known as *gatekeepers*; their decisions are based on several criteria:

• *Space*: Advertising has the highest priority. What is left in the paper is then the news "hole". This space must be allocated between local, national and international news.

• *Readership:* What audience is this paper trying to reach: urban, suburban or rural, professional or working class?

• *Physical requirements:* Despite the routine of putting a paper together, it still takes hours. Advertising is planned first, then major stories, and uneven or awkward spaces are used for "filler". Typography and aesthetics often determine the selection of a story. Editors try to keep related stories together, to visually balance photographs and headlines, and to achieve a good mix of live news and commentary.

The gatekeepers decide what is newsworthy, accurate, fair, objective, and in good taste. They must choose stories quickly, on the basis of intuition derived from long experience — and influenced by personal value systems. Any consciousness-raising that has been done with them will subtly affect these value systems and, thus, the coverage that is provided.

What you should know about how the media operate

Your task, then, is to become familiar with the news process, deadlines, standards of good taste, and everything else that combines to make a unique product at a particular paper. Changes in policy negotiated through managerial editors will mean little if they are not incorporated by the gatekeepers into their own standards.

Gatekeepers and decision-makers in all branches of the news media share certain basic policies and standards that are fundamental to the way they do business, and that will determine their willingness to work with you. For example:

• Most are in business to make money but each is in a different financial position and thus each will react differently to a possible increase or (feared and threatened) decrease of audience.

• Each aims for a particular segment of the total possible readership. That segment may or may not include you. Most media aim for the largest audience possible but a few will try to limit their audience in order to make their advertising more cost-effective. The *Saturday Evening Post*, before it collapsed, pared its subscription list from 6.8 million to 3 million by dropping subscribers in less affluent areas. Advertisers didn't want to pay the extra cost to reach those readers.

• All media are in the business of disseminating some kind of information. It may be hard news, or it may be feature material or entertainment. Each has a different balance, and a different set of values that determines what *is* news.

• All have their own standard procedures for obtaining material.
• All have their own paid staff.
• All have publishers and editors at the top who decide on editorial policies.
• All — while their editorial positions on issues may be rigid and long-standing — are capable of accepting change.
• All react more or less to what their audience thinks. Some won't admit it.
• All have moral and ethical standards, even if they aren't the ones you think they should have.
• Most have employees — reporters, editors, even gate-keepers — who are more liberal, or more conservative, than the policy-makers at the top.
• Each has a different policy on accepting free-lance and outside work.
• Most are open to your ideas if you take the right approach.

All of these factors have implications for your work with the media. As you come to better understand how the gatekeepers at a particular newspaper or broadcast station make their decisions, you'll be in a better position to tell when those decisions are reasonable, and when they represent an arbitrary or homophobic judgment.

Newsworthiness

Editors are usually highly knowledgeable about their jobs. They may take exception to your suggestion that they are consistently misjudging what ought to be run as legitimate news. So your first hurdle may be simply to establish that *we are news*. Stories about gay and lesbian issues *do* interest a large number of people.

If you've been watching the paper carefully, you may have found double standards about what gets coverage. Specific examples will carry more weight than a complaint.

Suppose a paper or station never carries news about passage of civil rights legislation in other cities and states. The editor's position is that such events are not news except where they happen. But the same paper or station ran stories about the *defeat* of a similar bill elsewhere. You must impress upon the editor the fact that such stories are not only important to lesbians and gay men, but also that reading only the coverage of bad news will influence the attitudes of the entire media audience.

Similarly, a paper's double standard is showing when it fails to cover a Lesbian and Gay Pride Week march but does run a page-one account of a homecoming parade. Does the editor understand that everybody participating in the gay march is risking their personal safety, a risk not shared by the homecoming participants? There *is* a news story here: that more and more people are willing to publicly identify themselves as gay.

So *you* must prod the media to re-evaluate their standards of what is news. You'll do that by getting to know editors and reporters, providing them with story and news ideas, and serving as role models for them, especially if they don't know any gay men or lesbians.

Keep track of media contacts

Put together a file of **institution cards** with vital information about the media organizations and their personnel. This file should operate in tandem with your clippings file, enabling you to measure your progress and plan further strategy. The cards will need regular updating; there's a high turnover of people in media.

Media advocacy groups should have a stable address, if only a box number that is checked frequently, and a telephone where someone can usually be reached. If the *Daily Planet* wants your comment on the story that Superman just came out, they want the comment *now* — not this evening when you get home and turn on your answering machine.

Organizations should have the same people or liaisons handle the same station, paper, or editor. This avoids confusion, and helps establish relationships of trust and familiarity that will make a big difference in the long run. Personal, one-to-one contacts will prove tremendously important in the long run.

Reporters

To establish contact with reporters or editors, send a memo of introduction to a department supervisor or editor asking for time to meet them after deadline.The request should be for no more than two of you, preferably a man and a woman. Initially you may have to go through one of the managerial editors with whom you first met.

There are three types of reporters: beat, general assignment and special assignment. Beat reporters are stationed at those places — city hall, the courts, police headquarters — that regularly generate news. General assignment reporters handle news stories that are not generated on beats. Special assignment reporters concentrate on general fields of interest like sports, legislation, science and religion.

Ideally the local gay community, if it is large, diverse and active enough, deserves a special assignment reporter of its own. A few stations, papers and magazines do have reporters who cover gay stories, among others, on a regular basis. If you've gotten this far, you know who the reporters are and you should begin by talking to them. But move cautiously. Those reporters who are sympathetic have probably been harassed for not being "objective" or may be suspected of being gay themselves. You might first invite them to meet with you or your organization. They can provide invaluable information and advice.

Although you may want a special-assignment reporter to cover gay events, you'll probably get general-assignment people. This can actually be an advantage. The gatekeeping process begins with reporters in the field as they decide what is, and is not, worth reporting. Like everyone else in the world, they will need educating too.

What if the media come to you?

With persistence you will not only expand the media's definition of what is news, you will also establish yourself as a reliable source of information, perhaps even one of the experts they like to quote. To encourage this attitude you and your group must keep pace with news and trends. Develop, like newsrooms themselves have done, contingency plans for otherwise-unexpected news, such as an important person coming out, a Supreme Court ruling, a murder, fire, raid or arrest, so that if your opinion is sought you will have something substantial to say.

Reporters may call with a question, to check a fact, to clarify a position, or to get an opinion. They'll be working under deadline pressures. Know your facts, and be prepared to respond specifically. Check on the position your group will take, as you will likely be quoted on their behalf.

If you can't answer on the spot, don't fudge. Just say, "I don't know but I can find out for you. How soon do you need an answer?" *Always call back, if only to report your inability to get the information.* You will add to your credibility and usefulness if you return calls quickly and can, much more often than not, provide complete answers.

When called, give an accurate answer even if it temporarily puts you or the community in an unfavorable light. This is tough. The instinct is to cover up or present an account in which you really don't believe. Never lie. It is the reporter's job to detect falsehoods, and your continued credibility can hinge on what you say.

Inreach

Once you have some experience in working with the media, you'll have gained knowledge that others can use. You might want to spread this information through what LAGMA calls "inreach" — reaching into our own community to raise consciousness, increase expectations of the media, and teach media skills. Inreach can be done informally by talking with your friends, comparing observations of media coverage and encouraging each other to write letters.

Inreach can be done more formally, by arranging to speak at meetings of other gay and lesbian organizations. LAGMA has spoken to a number of groups; we find that one of the most effective presentations is to briefly present some of the issues (such as are described in chapter four), and then to have an open discussion in which members of the group are encouraged to talk about what they've seen or heard in the media, and how they might respond. It's a good idea to take along sample copies of letters of praise and protest that you've written to the media, and perhaps one or two articles from the mainstream press to get the discussion started. Pamphlets such as the National Gay Task Force's "What gay people can do about the media" which can be ordered from their New York City office, or a brochure your own group has prepared, will be helpful. You might also take along copies of this book.

8. A Publicity Primer

"Freedom of the press belongs to those who own one" said media critic A.J. Liebling. Good press coverage, fortunately, needn't be quite so expensive; more important than having money is knowing what you're doing.

Public Relations (PR) is the art of using the media to inform and influence the public. PR is synonymous in the minds of many people with the legendary media campaigns by large corporations or big-time politicians to convince us to like junk-food desserts and junk-head presidents. But public relations can also help you:
• Educate the public about a commonly misunderstood subject;
• Get more people to participate in an event you're planning;
• Create public support for a position you have taken;
• Apply pressure to a recalcitrant government official;
• Raise money for your cause;
• Raise consciousness within the gay community; and
• Attract new members for your organization.
   Good PR can be used by all kinds of organizations — from a gay youth group to a Dignity (gay Catholics) organization or a lesbian mothers' support group — to achieve these goals. One or two people should be designated to coordinate PR and to act as liaisons with the media. As they

build up contacts at the local newspapers and broadcast stations, and develop their PR skills, these people will become increasingly effective.

This chapter describes some of the standard techniques and tools that you may find useful in presenting your message to the media. They include:

The Press Release — a story, written in the proper style, about an event you have planned or your stand on some issue, or some other news item.

Backgrounder — similar to a press release but with background information instead of news, often used to accompany a press release or as part of a press kit.

Press advisory — similar to a backgrounder, but focusing attention specifically on possible complications or pitfalls in the coverage of a specific story.

Public service announcement (PSA) — a short (usually two or three sentence) announcement that describes an event you have planned or a service you offer, directed at the broadcast media.

Press conference — an event in which you invite the press to hear representatives of your group talk about a specific issue and provide them with an opportunity to ask questions.

This chapter also gives some guidelines for generating material for the media:

• Handling the media work for a demonstration, march, or rally;

• Planning events for the specific purpose of getting publicity;

• Proposing feature story ideas to the press;

• Helping photographers and camera crews get the shots they need;

• Getting representatives of your group onto talk shows.

A Press List

Your first publicity-related job will be to compile a press list of all local print and electronic media, news and talk shows, and wire service offices. As this list is built up, it will eventually have a wealth of information about each one: address and phone number, deadlines, types of material they do and do not like, names of contacts there and a rundown of how helpful each is likely to be. As you monitor the media, you'll gain more information about each of these individuals.

Now you're ready to make news.

The Press Release

The standard tool for presenting information to the media is the press release. Sometimes these will be used verbatim by the media; other times they'll be rewritten or will serve as a take-off point for a reporter to get more information and do a longer story. And most often, they'll go right in the trash.

You can improve your chances of getting into one of the first two categories by giving them a truly interesting and newsworthy story, well-written, that follows the proper format:

• Use only one side of a sheet of standard 8½ by 11" paper, leaving at least a one-inch margin on all sides. Your release must be typed and it must be double- or triple-spaced.

• In the upper left or right corner type the date, your group's name (unless you're using a letterhead) and the name, address and phone number of a spokesperson who is easily reached by phone.

• A little further down, write "For immediate release." If you are sending a story out before it should appear, you should instead write "For release on" followed by the release date. Never give different release dates to different media.

• In capital letters, type a headline that briefly captures the important news angle of the story. The paper isn't likely to run your headline, but it will help the editor see what the story is about.

• Try to limit yourself to one page, two at the most. If you go over one page, write "MORE" at the bottom of each page except the last one. Additional pages should have your organization's name and the page number at the top. At the

ALYSON PUBLICATIONS, Inc.

P.O. Box 2783, Boston, Massachusetts 02208 • 617-542-5679

for more information, contact Ann Heron

FOR IMMEDIATE RELEASE

"A.I.D. CAN BE EASY," RESEARCHERS SAY

Artificial insemination by donor (AID) needn't be the complicated procedure that the health profession often makes it out to be. For lesbians who wish to become mothers, AID can be done at home safely and easily if just a few precautions are followed.

Those are the conclusions of Gillian Hanscombe and Jackie Forster, authors of the forthcoming book Rocking the Cradle: Lesbian Mothers, a Challenge in Family Living. The book is based on their interviews with lesbian mothers of all ages and backgrounds, and provides the most comprehensive look ever at how and why lesbians become mothers, and the social problems facing those who do.

AID was first used for women who could not get pregnant through heterosexual intercourse. For these women, lab tests and medical help were necessary in combination with AID, explain Hanscombe and Forster. But for lesbians who have no fertility problems, AID is easy and medical help is unnecessary. Although accurate figures are unavailable, they estimate that millions of children have now been conceived by AID.

All that's needed is close attention to a few important details: selecting the right donor, applying AID at the right time of the month, and using the most effective insemination techniques. The authors explain these procedures in detail in Rocking the Cradle. They also announce one unexpected finding of their research: for reasons that no one understands, some 80% of the children born through AID are boys.

Rocking the Cradle will be published this Mother's Day by Alyson Publications. Interested readers can find it in bookstores, or may order it by mail for $5.95 plus 75 cents postage from Alyson Publications, PO Box 2783, Boston, Mass. 02208.

-30-

Sample press release; this one was aimed at gay and feminist newspapers end of the release, skip a line then type, centered, "-30-" or "END".

• Include all the important facts — who, what, where, why, when — as early in the story as possible.

• Proofread carefully for both spelling and grammatical mistakes. An editor who's being distracted by misspellings or accidentally omitted words won't have much attention left for the content of your release — and will figure it's not worth much attention anyway.

• Be sure your release is going to the right editor or department. Call and ask if you aren't sure.

• Observe deadlines.

Backgrounders

As gay men and lesbians, we take for granted a lot of ideas that a reporter may never have heard of. A backgrounder helps to bridge that gap. It gives information, analysis and explanation that a reporter may use as a sidebar or supplement to the main story, or that may simply help the reporter do a more accurate job on the main story. A backgrounder will most likely be written in a style similar to the press release, with important information at the top, development in the middle, details at the end.

Suppose a bill is pending at city hall that would ban job discrimination based on sexual orientation; you're about to mail out a press release announcing your group's support for the bill. A backgrounder could name other cities where such laws are already on the books. It could also explain, for example, that the term "gay civil rights" is preferable to just "gay rights" because the first term makes it clear that such legislation only provides us the protection that other people already have. You could also search out, and name, accepted churches, unions, and organizations that support the proposed bill.

(By the way, a gay organization coming out in favor of a gay civil rights bill isn't likely to be deemed newsworthy by anyone. If you'll invest the time and creativity to come up with a better news angle, it will be well rewarded.)

Press advisories

In December of 1977, Bostonians opened their morning papers to read about a boy sex ring involving dozens of local gay men. For months the case stayed in the headlines. It was time for a press advisory.

An advisory is written more in the style of a letter or memo, rather than as a press release. It is not intended for publication, it's simply an effort to draw the media's attention to the potential pitfalls in the coverage of such a story. In this case, a group called the Boston/Boise Committee issued an excellent set of suggestions for media handling of such cases. "Avoid the use of obviously biased words such as 'prey', 'sex den', 'sordid'," they advised. "Do not publish statements of unidentified sources without checking them out; this is especially true for details which will never have to be disproven or proven in the court." The full text of this advisory appears in the Appendix.

Statements to the Press

If you are responding to a spontaneous or late-breaking event like a Supreme Court ruling or a sudden series of arrests, you can't afford the delay of writing, copying, and mailing out a press release. Draft a brief (two or three sentence) statement and phone it — slowly — to the news desk.

Public Service Announcements

Public Service Announcements (PSA's) are short messages that announce public events or services. By FCC rules, the broadcast media must set aside a certain amount of free air time for PSA's that are submitted by non-profit organizations.

In general, PSA's cannot directly ask for money, solicit group membership, or advocate a particular candidate. Beyond that, different stations have different standards as to what constitutes an acceptable PSA; some will avoid announcements they deem controversial. If a station rejects your PSA on such grounds, you can request a meeting with the station manager to explore the problem.

Stations tend to run PSA's at times when they're short on paid advertisements; or when they need material to fill out a program's time slot. So PSA's are more often broadcast late at night or early in the morning, rather than during prime time.

The volume of PSA's received by any one station, especially in a metropolitan area, is usually greater than they can use, and only a small percentage of the PSA's received may actually be aired. If you feel your announcement is crucial, and if you have strings to pull — that is, if you have met and know the station manager or another responsible person — then pull them. Remind him or her of the community ascertainment survey or editorial board meeting you participated in. You can also increase the chances of your PSA being broadcast by following the proper submission procedures.

The format and method for submitting a PSA will vary slightly from station to station, so call the Public Service Director before sending anything in. In general, the following guidelines apply:

• Submit the material about two weeks in advance, and follow up with a phone call.

• Keep it short. PSA's generally run from ten to thirty seconds, but the shorter ones are most likely to be aired. Use simple words, and give only vital information: who, what, when, where, why and how.

• For radio, submit the copy in writing (some stations may prefer a taped copy, or may want the information submitted on their own forms), double- or triple-spaced on your letterhead or on blank 8½ × 11 paper, with the name and phone number of a contact person. Indicate the approximate time, allowing roughly two or two and a half words per second.

• Television stations may prefer sound-on-film, videotape, or glass slides. Again, contact the station's Public Service Director to see what format is acceptable. Television stations will often help with the production.

The Gay Speakers Bureau
P.O. Box 2232, Boston, MA 02107. 617-354-0133

June 2, 1982

Contact: Pat Galloway
354-0133

PUBLIC SERVICE ANNOUNCEMENT   (20 seconds)

The Gay Speakers Bureau provides lesbians and gay men as speakers

to groups who want to know more about what it's like to be gay. To

request speakers for your church, synagogue, service organization,

high school or college class, or other group, call the Bureau at

354-0133.

Sample public service announcement

Press conferences

Press conferences are to be saved for truly "hard news" events or issues, such as Jerry Falwell coming to town to launch a campaign against a gay civil rights bill. They are a lot of bother to put together; before you schedule a press conference ask yourself: couldn't this thing be handled as well through a press release, or by talking to a single reporter?

The media must be convinced that a press conference is worth their time before they'll attend. If you know some reporters or editors, ask their advice. Never assume that everyone you ask will come; a couple of drop-outs are to be expected. Should there be many no-shows, however, not only will the press conference fail but the people who do come will be irritated at you and with themselves. Any future conference will be all the harder to arrange.

Before you decide to go ahead with a press conference, be sure you have enough people to do all the work that will be involved. We recommend that at least one or two of these be people who have had past experience in setting up press conferences.

Ideally, the "call" for a press conference is announced three or four days in advance through a written format such as a press release or advisory. If you're calling for a conference in an emergency, telephone the news desk and the reporters of your choice. A sample format for a call is:

(Who) This is − − from − −.

(Where/When) I'm calling to tell you that we're holding a press conference at 10:00 a.m. on Tuesday, March 6, at 64 Front Street to announce our plans for responding to the latest New Right campaign.

(Who) The following people will speak: − −. The conference is sponsored by a coalition of organizations, including − −.

(Special Fact) This will be the first public announcement by any group on this subject.

(Easy access to you) If you need to reach me, my name is − −. The number here is − −. Do you have any questions?

News conferences should only be announced when the logistical details are known: where the conference will take place, what day and time, and who will be present to speak. Contingency planning for a publicity campaign should include a strategy for setting up a conference in case the need suddenly arises.

If you do have time to notify the media in writing, be sure to telephone follow-ups the afternoon before a morning conference, or the morning before an afternoon conference. When the electronic media are present, the timing of the conference is especially important. If the local evening news is presented at 6 p.m., hold the conference between 9 a.m. and 3 p.m. If this is impossible, aim for the late evening news at 10 or 11 p.m. by holding the conference between 7 and 9 p.m. Target the daily newspaper deadlines as well — though this juggling can admittedly get quite complicated — by holding the conference three to five hours before the afternoon deadline.

The best days to hold a conference, as far as getting newspaper coverage, are Monday, Tuesday and Wednesday. The Thursday paper's priority is advertising for the weekend; Friday's is features and weekend events. Your conference will have a better chance of making the papers on a "slow news day" when news is relatively scarce; these are somewhat unpredictable, but you can at least avoid times when you know another event will be competing with you for media attention.

Certain technical arrangements must be made in preparation for a conference.

• Provide space large enough to accommodate all the people expected to attend. However, slightly cramped quarters can be better than too much room, because crowded places give the impression that "everyone wants to be there." Be familiar with the room: know the location of electrical outlets, telephones, fire extinguishers and alarms, exits, and restrooms.

• Avoid holding a press conferences outdoors unless there is a good reason to do so. The sound pickup on microphones will be "windy" and muted and the weather is, of course, unpredictable.

• Assemble press kits for reporters. These will be large envelopes or folders with pocket inserts, giving such information as:

— The agenda;
— A list of participants with titles, identification and biographies;
— Backgrounders if appropriate;
— Copies of formal statements and speeches that will be made;
— Other relevant information such as a brochure or photos — but keep it to a minimum.

• Provide a sign-in sheet for reporters so you'll have a record of who attended. This information can be transferred to your press list.

• Greet the attendees at the door and have someone appointed to hand each one a press kit and sign them in. Advise them of speakers who will be available for comments or interviews after the conference has ended, and offer yourself as a reference for any question or problems.

• Arrange the seating for the conference so that newspaper reporters can be seated in the first two rows. If you can, provide tables for writers. Leave a wide aisle down the middle of the seating for still photographers, and a wider aisle between the front and back row of seats where the technical crews can place cameras and recording devices.

• Speakers should be at the front of the room, preferably on a dais or behind a podium (and in front of some sort of backdrop that will cover distracting background material like ugly pipes, blackboards, etc.)

The conference itself must be enacted carefully. Start on time if possible; never more than fifteen minutes late. If most of the media that's expected has arrived, start things rolling and hope that anyone else who's interested will show up in time to still get some good coverage.

Your portion of the press conference should ideally be fifteen to thirty minutes long, with no more than five speakers scheduled. Speakers should try to speak for about two to five minutes each, and copies of their statements should be available to the press before the conference. Rehearse beforehand, anticipating the questions that will come.

One spokesperson should moderate the conference, introducing the speakers, moving the agenda along, opening the conference to questions from the press. This person should know when and how to interrupt and who to select as questioners, and will have to judge when to end the conference.

Expect the unexpected. Be sure you know the name and number of the nearest hospital. Some homophobes might take exception to your plans if word gets out, and try to disrupt the conference. In that case, you'll be instantly forgotten as all eyes, ears and equipment turn in their direction. Plan in advance how such an interruption might be handled, so that you can win back the media's attention.

After the press conference, monitor the media to check up on the reporting of the event, and respond accordingly with letters and phone calls.

Staging an event

Demonstrations, marches and rallies will be more effective if you get the best possible media coverage for them. Appoint one person to coordinate press activities for the event. This should *not* be a speaker or anyone else who already has other responsibilities; it's a job in itself. This coordinator will have many of the same responsibilities as the coordinator for a press conference.

• Prepare plenty of press kits, giving background information, a statement on why the event is necessary, names of spokespersons and a phone number that a reporter can call afterwards for more information. If you can include copies of any speeches being made, reporters will be more likely to

get their quotes right and camera crews will be more likely
to start the film rolling right before the high point of a
speech. Also include advance notice of any events that will
lend themselves to picture-taking.

• Arrive early, and become familiar with traffic patterns,
lighting systems, availability of electrical outlets, location
of the fuse box, of telephones, and so on.

• Greet the press as you give them their kits. Reporters
should all know who the coordinator is, in case they need
information or technical assistance. Either take the name
and affiliation of each reporter or have them sign in at a
special table.

• Encourage everyone who is likely to be approached by
the media to have a short, quotable line already planned
out.

• Provide good ideas for both newspaper and TV picture
coverage. At a march, for example, you might know of a
spot where photographers can stand to get a picture that
shows the true size of the crowd. Tell them about it; they'll
appreciate the tip and you'll get coverage that more
accurately shows your true strength.

At some events, certain participants will not want their
picture to appear in the paper or on television. At private
functions you can try to control this; the *Gay Community
News*, at a community meeting held after its offices were
destroyed by fire, posted one side of the room PHOTOS OK and
the other side NO PHOTOS. They explained to the media what
was going on, and everybody was happy.

In more public situations, you can only hope to persuade the media to act responsibly. In any case, send a
written explanation *beforehand* to the media, pointing out
that in the absence of non-discrimination laws, many
people would stand to lose jobs, housing or child custody if
they were publicly identified as lesbian or gay. Explain that
you will make arrangements at the event for them to be able
to photograph people who are willing to be publicly

identified, and request that they not take other pictures. Then, on the day of the event, meet them at the door to repeat the explanation and request.

Most press photographers will bridle at any suggestion that they restrict their activities. Your best bet is to clearly explain in advance why you are making such a request, and be sure to provide good photo opportunities of people who are willing subjects.

Pseudo-events

Many of the news stories you read in the paper are not about real news events at all, but are about pseudo-events, specifically planned for the media by someone who wants publicity for something. The media are surprisingly receptive to such stunts; all you need to take advantage of this receptivity is some imagination.

In the 1950s, the French cognac industry wanted to boost its U.S. sales. A public relations agency arranged a series of pseudo-events; one of these stunts was to get a French chef onto the Jack Paar show to create the world's biggest crepe suzette, doused with a gallon of French cognac. In a six-year period, U.S. sales of cognac nearly tripled.

In 1970, the Chicago Area Draft Resisters (CADRE) was looking for ways to let the public know of their existence as an anti-draft group. They decided to give an award to General Hershey, then director of the Selective Service. The award: a copy of Dr. Seuss's book *Yertle the Turtle*, about a turtle who make all the other turtles stand on top of one another so that he could stand on top of them all. Yertle ultimately took a fall when the bottom turtle burped. The story had just the right combination of irony and humor and it got citywide publicity for CADRE.

After the 1980 presidential election, third-party candidate Barry Commoner complained in the *Columbia Journalism Review* that the media had ignored his most important statements on major public issues. "Bill Zimmerman, my campaign manager, suggested that dealing with the national media was like talking to a mule: first you had to hit it over the head with a two-by-four to get its attention. With that thought in mind, he suggested a radio commercial starting out with a word that some newspapers quaintly refer to as a 'barnyard epithet.'" Commoner reluctantly did so, and the result was spectacular: "In two days the Citizens Party received more news stories and broadcast time than it had received in its entire history." The *Detroit Free Press*, which had completely ignored Commoner's plan for revitalizing the auto industry, ran a front-page story about the commercial.

As you monitor the media, you'll often see "news" stories that are clearly the result of conscious PR work by a group. Use these for inspiration and for ideas. What could your group do to draw media attention to an important issue in a novel way?

Suggesting feature stories

A feature story is one that isn't tied to a specific news event; features may be written or taped weeks before they appear. Features are run because the editor thinks they will interest readers. Your job is to come up with a story idea that combines this editorial need — to entertain readers — with your goal of increasing public awareness.

Make a list of such story ideas, and for each write down why it would make an interesting story, and who a reporter could contact to get started on it. This list can be submitted when you meet with a newspaper or broadcast station. Don't count on them to follow through on it though; you'll undoubtedly have to keep working on them.

Try to identify the reporters who seem most likely to develop your ideas well. If you're monitoring the media already, you'll have a good sense of this. Then, send a letter to both the department or feature editor and to the reporter you have selected, letting each know of the letter to the other. End the letter by saying you'll phone in a few days to see if such a story would appeal to them.

When you do call, be courteous and ready to supply extra facts. The reporter may be intelligent but unfamiliar with gay issues, and may need help in seeing the value of your story. Try to come up with the strongest possible angle — the approach to the story that makes it unusual, newsworthy, interesting.

If your proposal is rejected, thank the reporter or editor for their time, and note their name, the idea, the date, and salient points of the conversation. This will further build up your press file, so that you'll have an increasingly accurate sense of who to approach on any specific idea.

You can also write an article yourself and submit it. Find out what the policies are, at the magazines and newspapers for which you might write, regarding free-lance submissions. A talk with the editor before you begin writing could help you take the approach most likely to be accepted.

It's easier to get a free-lance article published if you're an established writer, but that's not an essential qualification. It *is* essential that you have good writing skills; double-check all facts, names, and figures; and present your article in the style required by the publication it's going to.

Photographs

Too many people still think that all gay men walk around in either dresses or leather all day, and that all lesbians can be identified by a "mannish" appearance. They need to see more accurate images of us in the media, images that show our diversity. A picture *is* worth a thousand words if it breaks down previously-held stereotypes.

Before the lesbian and gay pride march, your press kit should include an advisory memo explaining that if photographers direct their cameras only at the most flamboyant while ignoring the ordinary, they are giving an inaccurate and misleading portrayal of the event. Similar advisories can be issued before other events that might lend themselves to stereotyped picture-taking.

When you're planning any type of public event, think about whether it provides good opportunities for photographers. Is the lighting adequate? Will too much clutter show up? Is there a way you could create an unusual picture opportunity?

You can also supply the media with your own photographs, by themselves or accompanying a press release. Smaller publications frequently need graphics and will welcome a story that includes its own pictures. Try to supply interesting action shots; avoid cliched and over-used poses when possible.

The prints you supply should be 8 × 10 or 5 × 7 black-and-white glossies. Don't write directly on the back or paperclip anything to the photo, or you will mar the finish; the best way to attach a caption is to type it onto a gummed label, then stick it to the back of the photo.

Your caption should include complete information about the picture: who, what, where, when and why. If people are shown, identify them left to right: their names and affiliations. If you are tempted to use a pithy little one-liner for impact, use it as a headline over a caption that includes full information. Try to match the caption's style to the one prevailing at the newspaper. Photos should have strong contrast and be of the best possible quality. Where possible, be sure to credit the photographer. Whenever you send photographs through the mail, you must include a cardboard stiffener in the envelope.

An especially ambitious group might want to develop a photo file, showing gay people in a variety of contexts. Be sure you keep accurate records about where each photo was taken and who's in it. If the media know you have such a file, they may come to you for pictures; you'll thus be sure they're getting good material, and you'll reinforce your image as a useful, professional source of news material.

Talk and interview shows

Talk shows and other TV and radio feature shows commonly handle controversial subjects. Participation in a community ascertainment or any other formal meeting with station management can make it easier for you to arrange programs; such meetings will speed up the process of discovering what people, and what stations, are most likely to be receptive to you.

The list of feature story ideas you developed for newspapers will also be useful for broadcast media. Which of these stories could be developed especially well on the air? Who is available to talk on these subjects? Guests must be willing to come out publicly; they should also be reasonably articulate and comfortable with the idea of talking about gay issues on the air. It's helpful to rehearse any appearance: have another person take the role of moderator and ask questions, giving the guest practice in replying quickly and intelligently. Make a list of the questions most likely to come up; for predictable questions you can decide in advance what is a good way to make your point.

Booking: Once you've got a topic, speakers, and a possible station in mind, call the station and ask who books the show in which you are interested. Write to that person, explaining your idea and why it would be interesting to a predominantly straight audience. Soon afterward, follow up with a phone call. All this should be done at least two or three weeks before you want the appearance.

If you'd like to have your group's name and phone number flashed on the screen during your appearance, this is the time to bring that up. Many stations will be happy to accommodate such a request, but only if they have a week or so to prepare the sign.

If your idea is turned down, try again in a few weeks with another idea. If a station consistently turns down your ideas for what seem to be homophobic reasons, then it's time to try to meet with them.

The show: Before a call-in show, let the gay community know it's coming up and get them on the phones. Use calls to supplement what is being said on the show, or to lead the speakers into a new subject area — it's hard for an inexperienced person to sense the overall flow of a conversation while in the middle of it, and someone listening may be able to get things onto a better track with a phone call.

One way to avoid getting sidetracked is to identify, before the show, the one or two key points you want to make, and practice ways to articulate them. Then watch for opportunities to fit those points in as you answer questions. Practice this with someone and soon you'll have no trouble including your key points in the answers to almost any questions you could be asked.

Avoid organized debates. It's hard enough to make the points you want when an impartial moderator is questioning you; it can be impossible when you're being interrupted and your ideas are being misquoted by a hostile opponent, who may well have considerable public speaking experience. If the station explains that "We want to represent both sides of this controversial issue of public importance," you can maintain that civil rights are not controversial, and point out that the KKK is not normally invited to "balance" a presentation of black people's civil rights, nor are Nazis invited to "balance" the opinions of Jews. Or, you could just explain that you don't see how you can clearly present your ideas in such a highly-charged, prejudiced environment.

If the station is resolved on a debate or a devil's advocate format (in which the host is the opponent), you may decide to go along rather than get no exposure. If you do, be sure your representative is unusually articulate and fast-thinking, and familiar with the arguments and objections likely to be advanced by the opposition.

You'll also want to get equal representation of lesbians and gay men. Resist moves on the part of the producer to focus only on male issues. In a debate, if your opponents try to ignore lesbians, you should not only prevent this from happening, you can also point out what they are doing, and what it means.

On the air: Avoid wearing white or brightly colored clothes on television; jewelry can also be distracting because it will glitter. Don't smoke or engage in nervous movements like swiveling in your chair. For a radio show the host will demonstrate how best to speak into the microphone; try not to make extraneous sounds near the mike like rustling papers or lighting a match.

During the show, repeatedly mention the name of your organization, even the phone number and address if you can. You just may be throwing a lifeline to a few highly closeted gays in the audience.

It's the job of the host to inject excitement or controversy into the show; your previous monitoring will tell you what to expect. There's a good chance you'll be asked some questions that are hostile — or that are so ignorant they seem hostile. Avoid the temptation to return that hostility. You might win the argument with the questioner, but you'll lose thousands of viewers. Maintaining a calm, sensible image will be far more productive. If a question is really bigoted, point that fact out, then re-phrase the question before answering.

As you speak, remember that while your host may or may not be well-informed, that's not your real audience. You're really speaking to thousands of listeners at home — a diverse and generally naive group. Start with the basics, and avoid insider-talk. Even terms like "coming out" will be unfamiliar to many people in your audience. Quote authoritative sources to refute the myths that many people have. In your conversation, don't assume that your audience knows anything true about homosexuality.

After the show: Talk to the host and station manager about how it went. They may have suggestions that will help you be more effective next time.

If you feel the show did some good, tell them. Mention, for example, that for the many gay teenagers who could have tuned in, this show might have helped to lessen their feeling of isolation. *Positive reinforcement is important* for

producers who do shows with good gay content. Your ene-
mies will be sure to phone in plenty of complaints, and you
must do your best to counteract that.

9. Now Go Buy a Hundred Postcards

We've said a lot in this book about what you can do to influence the media. Some of it is simple, some of it isn't. Certain things can be done most effectively by an organized media group.

But real change in the media will only come when thousands of gay men and lesbians take *individual responsibility* for talking back to the media. The average reporter or newscaster may only get two or three letters about the coverage provided by a particular story. If one of those letters is from you, you'll be in a position to influence that reporter's thinking. With just one or two postcards or letters a week, and not more than ten minutes of your time, you can have far more influence than you thought possible. In fact, if each of us just wrote one letter or postcard a *month* the impact would be enormous. Think about it!

The National Rifle Association, for example, recently ran a full-page ad that featured an eight-year-old boy who is an NRA member. *McCall's* magazine ran the ad in several of its regional editions, and got about five condemnatory letters according to Ray Eyes, the publisher. Those five letters were enough to change the magazine's policy. "We will not run [another NRA] ad with children," said Eyes.

The important thing is to actually get those letters written. We suggest that right now you go out and buy a

hundred postcards, or better yet, a hundred sets of stationery with envelopes and stamps. Keep them with a pen
next to the chair where you read the paper or watch TV.
Next time something offends you, send a complaint to the
offender. And if you hear good coverage about our lives,
send them a compliment! Remember, there are many
homophobes out there who will be sure to send in an objec-
tion when lesbian and gay issues are presented in a positive
light. Make sure our voices are heard, too.

It won't take long to get down the basic information:
the date of the show or article; what offended or pleased
you; and why it did so. With practice you can have the note
finished by the time the commercial break is over.

Addresses for national networks and certain national
magazines are at the end of this book. They're followed by
several blank pages on which you can record the addresses
of the local media that you follow most closely. *Write those
addresses down now!* If you have addresses, pen and paper,
envelopes and stamps all handy in one place, it'll be much
easier to get a letter off quickly when you want to.

Still got some extra energy? You can be even more
effective with a couple more minutes of effort. Before you
write, phone the place you're about to write to. Tell them
that you were offended or pleased by such-and-such story,
and ask who you should write to about it. The comments
you make over the phone may be relayed to the appropriate
person; then you'll make an additional impact when your
letter arrives. And if you know you're not going to write, at
least get in the habit of telephoning with your compliments
and complaints. Let them know that we are here.

For three years, as the Lesbian and Gay Media Advocates,
we've been working to get more and better coverage of our
lives. We've seen some real improvements in that time, but
whenever we're about to pat ourselves on our collective
back, the station or paper that we thought had become so
sensitive to our concerns will do something outrageous.
There's still a long road ahead. We shouldn't be satisfied

until the public has discarded old associations and comes to view our lives in a new light. Join us by learning to talk back to the media.

Appendices 1 and 2:

Sample Letters and Story Ideas

On the next several pages are samples of letters that LAGMA members and others have sent to the media. They are followed by a copy of the story ideas that we prepared for some of our first meetings with local newspapers. Although you won't want to copy any of this material word-for-word, parts of it may be useful in your own work.

```
        Sal Micciche
        Ombudsman
        The Boston Globe
        Boston, Mass.

        Dear Mr. Micciche:

        In the March 16 Sunday Globe, on page
        28 in the Metro/Region section, appeared
        the enclosed ad. As a gay man, I find
        Question 1 in this ad particularly
        offensive. Had the question been, "Do
        you approve of known practicing Jews
        teaching in public schools?" instead
        of homosexuals, would you have printed
        the ad?

        Does the Globe have a policy regarding
        how to decide whether to run a potentially
        offensive advertisement? If so I would be
        interested in seeing it.

                        Sincerely,


                        R. Andrews
```

Alan Richman
The Boston Globe
Boston, Mass. 02107

Dear Mr. Richman,
    Your column of July 8, "Red, White and Gay," is remarkable for
its insulting and insensitive attitude toward the lesbian and gay
community. Though you adopt the stance of a bemused observer, your
cynical use of innuendo and caricature renders your "observations"
somewhat less than humorous.
    In the context of continuing oppression of lesbians and gays,
who enjoy none of the legal protection accorded to many other
minorities, you write: "Cherry Grove is the farthest extension of
our cherished American freedoms, the Bill of Rights all wrapped up
in a silver slave bracelet." Ever so subtly, you manage to imply:
(1) that the lesbians and gays of Cherry Grove, by excercising
their own rights, are abusing the rights of others, thus
"enslaving" the rest of the country; (2) that homosexuality, at
least in Cherry Grove, is synonymous with sado-masochism.
    Perhaps you see the legitimate forms of self-expression and
interaction among members of this community as a threat to the
population at large. If so, you fail to provide any clear reasons
for such a view. Instead, you prefer to manipulate stereotypes.
Lesbians, according to you, are "older women" who "convince" (i.e.,
seduce) sweet young things by means of "constant caresses." Gay
men, in your eyes, "wriggle" and "shriek" and "care little for
motherhood." Listening to a Yankee game on the radio, it seems,
indicates heterosexuality.
    You may object that you were only reporting what you saw; that
your column refers not to the entire lesbian and gay community, but
only to one segment of that community. Yet throughout the column
one finds evidence of a desire both to see certain prejudices
confirmed, and to interpret Cherry Grove as a microcosm of lesbian
and gay society. By comparing the beach at Cherry Grove to "one of
those what's-wrong-with-this-picture" scenes, you allow the word
"wrong," with all its moralistic connotations, to resonate loudly
and clearly. What's "wrong," in your opinion, is that "only
occasionally does one see a person identifiable as being of the
straight persuasion."
    As I see it, Mr. Richman, what's wrong is not the scene, but
your attempt to portray it — and, by insinuation, the lives of all
lesbians and gay men — as aberrant, bizarre, and at the same time
stereotypically "amusing." Such journalistic irresponsibility seems
unworthy of a writer for the _Globe_, a newspaper that on the whole
has shown considerable intelligence in its treatment of the lesbian
and gay community.

                        Sincerely,

                        Lee Brown

January 15, 1980

Mike Barnicle
THE BOSTON GLOBE
Boston, Ma. 02107

Dear Mr. Barnicle:

Your January 7 article on Bert Parks being fired from the Miss
America Pageant relies on "humor" that is as destructive and
prejudiced as any racist humor would be.

You ask "Why not Truman Capote (as MC) -- he would be no problem in
the dressing room." Surely, you would never presume to ask: "Why
not Andrew Young, you couldn't see him in the backstage darkness?"
Humor based on demeaning another's sexual being is as ugly as that
which debases another's race. And your statement to "Get a real
queen and give the job to Paul Lynde" may not only be grounds to
precipitate a lawsuit but, again, is on the level of: "Get a real
Jew and give the job to..."

Such statements must be seen for what they are. Those who insist,
"Hey, these are just good-natured jibes!' overlook how they feel
when whatever group, religion, persuasion, minority or majority
they belong to is consciously and publicly mocked by others in
print. If such ridicule has occurred because you were unaware, then
you should now understand. We hope you see what we have pointed out
here.

                         Sincerely,

                         Susan Kildare

March 24, 1982

Ann Landers
c/o Wheeling News-Register
Wheeling, W.Va. 26003

Dear Ann,

I think you were correct to tell the reader
from New Jersey that you were going to keep
publishing letters about gay men and lesbians;
however, I think you <u>were</u> wrong to group lesbian
and gay concerns with "rape, incest, drug
addiction... et. al."

Homosexuality is <u>not</u> one of the seven plagues.
Those of us who are gay or who have family
members, friends or neighbors who are gay, we
who are homeowners, office workers, blue or white
collar workers, artists -- have made this society
infinitely more generous and richer than it could
be -- and have no place at all in the group of
"not very pretty problems" you mentioned.

Homosexuality: loving and returning the love of
someone of the same gender, is not a violent act,
but society's assumptions about it often are.

                        Sincerely,

                        Michelle Robinson

44 Main Street
Fernwood, Indiana
Feb. 26, 1982

Ann Landers
c/o The Lafayette Journal-Courier
Lafayette, Indiana

Dear Ann Landers,

Although I've always been impressed with your support
of gay civil rights, your February 26 column convinced me
that you still do not understand how gay people feel about
themselves. I think it is both illogical and unfair for
you to assume that most lesbians and gays are "wretched
and miserable" on the basis of your mail. The letters you
receive from gay men in search of help could hardly
provide a representative sampling of the gay community.
Since your job is to solve other people's problems, I
would be very much surprised if letters from "normal and
healthy" people outnumbered those from people with
problems.

I also think you do gays a disservice by labeling
homosexuality a "personality disorder" and comparing it to
a prejudice or an addiction. The first comparison implies
that gay people hate the members of the opposite sex, and
the second implies that gays are drunk on sex; both of
which are untrue.

I've enclosed a subscription form for Gay Community
News, one of the nation's most respected gay journals.
Although you probably have enough to read already, I hope
you subscribe to it. It will be useful in counseling
lesbians and gays, by giving you a broader perspective on
the issues and mood of the gay community.

Sign me: Glad to be Gay
Sincerely yours,

T.J. Owens

March 15, 1980

Hank Klibanoff
Timothy Dwyer
THE BOSTON GLOBE
Boston, Ma. 02107

Dear Messrs. Klibanoff & Dwyer:

We'd like to comment on the story which ran in the Wednesday,
March 5 GLOBE, entitled: "Lowell man names 2 in the '78 murder
of gay." Although this is a long and involved case, we found
your reporting to be accurate and fair, and the language used as
free from the negative bias which has - too often in the past -
been associated with stories that concern lesbians and gay men.

                           Best-

                           for LAGMA

cc: Editor/Metro & Region/GLOBE

February 14, 1981

Station Manager
WXKS —— Kiss 108 FM
99 Revere Beach Pkwy.
Medford, Mass.

Dear Station Manager,
    It was quite gratifying for me to listen to your
Valentine's Day program, which included messages from
several people to their partners, and to hear several
messages sent from men to other men, and women to other
women. In the course of my listening I heard only a few, but
this is a very positive and validating experience for the
tons of gay people who listen to your station. Since many
gay people do not realize that they have access like this to
your station, I urge you to sit down and do some solid
thinking about the way your station relates to many of its
gay listeners.
    While your news sometimes includes gay-related stories,
and generally they are well done, I recommend you consider
doing more positive outreach to the community: PSA's for gay
groups (particularly the gay youth group, many of whose
members listen to KISS 108 24 hours a day, 7 days a week),
more same-sex couples in events like today's Valentine's Day
treat, and perhaps a specific news program or discussion
show for lesbians and gay men. You really don't seem to
realize the vast audience you have; you could be doing a lot
more to satisfy that audience (though the music itself keeps
many of us happy). Still, positive efforts would be much
appreciated.
    Keep up the good work.

                        Sincerely,

                        Roger Erikson

cc: Lesbian & Gay Media Advocates

Lesbian and Gay Media Advocates

%o GCN 22 Bromfield Street Boston, Ma. 02108

STORY IDEAS FOR MEDIA COVERAGE
OF GAY AND LESBIAN
ISSUES

This list is by no means exhaustive, it is merely a beginning. There are many issues that gay men and lesbians have struggled for years to air that merit and warrant publication in your paper; both to raise our own expectations of fair coverage, and to sensitize heterosexual readers to the realities of our lives.

The lesbian and gay "issue" is no small one. It speaks to the profound question of whether this society can tolerate difference without equating it with deviance. To realize a progressive resolution of this question, your newspaper can be extremely instrumental -- not by taking sides, but by simply covering this side as well.

In general, we see potential coverage as being divided into three main areas: Human Interest; News; Arts and Culture.

I. HUMAN INTEREST

General Goals:

To present the diversity and reality of gay and lesbian experience; to document the difficulties faced by those for whom negative societal sanctions require the leading of a double-life; to document the complex process of "coming out"; to help readers who might be extremely isolated gain access to support and validation; to document the accomplishments of gay men and lesbians.

Specific Story Ideas:

1) A two or three part series of human interest portraits of various gay and lesbian individuals who must remain anonymous. Hopefully, the interview material will convey the many issues involved, as well as the personal compensations required. Possible subjects might include: a teacher, a mental health worker, a media person, a parent, an athlete.

2) An article (or several) documenting the complex and life-long process of coming out: to oneself, to one's parents, to one's children, to one's co-workers, to the public at large.

3) An article on gay and lesbian youth. Again, interviews with young gay people would convey the issue best. Also, coverage of the organizations run by and for gay youth.

4) An article on the widening participation of parents of gay people in civil rights advocacy.

Lesbian and Gay Media Advocates

c/o GCN 22 Bromfield Street Boston, Ma. 02108

Story Ideas
Page 2

5) A story tracing the history of the Gay Movement.

6) An article on the Gay Community News, the nation's oldest, most widely circulated gay newspaper (based here in Boston).

7) An article on gay and lesbian business-people.

8) Gay and lesbian couples in the suburbs, the rise of single, same sex home ownership - perhaps for the real estate section.

9) The gay and lesbian/feminist alternative health and mental health movement; i.e. women's therapy collectives.

10) An investigative report on how more traditional mental health facilities (hospitals, clinics, child guidance centers) are meeting the needs of the gay population.

11) Rape: an investigative report on the kinds of services provided by area hospitals to women in crisis.

12) Articles on Black and Third World lesbians and gay men - movements that have continued to struggle without recognition for many years.

13) Coverage of various gay and lesbian organizations which are concerned with improving social and legal conditions for gay people.

Resources:

We have picked a sampling of resources here which could be utilized to obtain information on many of the above-mentioned topics. In addition, the Quick Gay Guide of the Gay Community News is a rich source of information. We will keep you informed of new resources through updated lists.

Gay Speakers Bureau: a diverse group of individuals willing to be interviewed; 354-0133.

BAGALS (Boston Area Lesbian and Gay Schoolworkers): P.O Box 178, Astor Street, Boston, MA 02123.

Committee for Gay Youth: c/o GCN Box 10GY, 22 Bromfield Street, 02108.

Lesbian Liberation, c/o the Cambridge Women's Center which is an excellent resource Center for finding out about and contacting lesbian activists in the Boston area; 354-8807.

Lesbian and Gay Media Advocates

% GCN 22 Bromfield Street Boston, Ma. 02108

Story Ideas
Page 3

    El Comite Latino de Lesbiana y Homosexuals de Boston: 354-1755.

    The Conditions Five Collective: editors of the Black Women's Issue
       of _Conditions_, a feminist publication, many of whom live in
       Boston; through the Cambridge Women's Center.

    Lesbian and Gay Parents Project: 492-2655.

    The back pages of Sojourner's and Equal Times: 2 area feminist papers.

II. NEWS STORIES

General Goal:

To report news that either directly affects the lives of gay men and
lesbians, or the newsworthy activities of the gay community. In addition,
to include the gay and lesbian perspective as part of a larger, more
general article: such as, the fate of gay prisoners in a more general
article about the New Mexico prison uprising.

Specific Story Ideas:

1) A follow-up article on "queer-bashing" - this is not a one-shot
event - including the gay community's own response to this fact: for
example, a recent Gay Town Meeting on Violence, which drew more than
150 concerned lesbians and gay men.

2) Gay Civil Rights - both on a state and federal level. This might
entail a commentary on the prejudicial remarks made by legislators in
sessions, coverage of the National Gay Rights Lobby in Washington,
the efforts to pass a Gay Civil Rights Bill in Massachusetts.

3) The immigration laws covering gay people: are they discriminatory?

4) The ciritical issue of violence against women - covered not just
as a chronicle of violent incidents against women, but also coverage of
the innovative responses of feminist and lesbian feminist groups to this
fact. For example, an article about any one of the Green Light
Organizing efforts in Boston.

5) Politics: the activities of gay men and lesbians who hold office;
the attempts by politicians to appeal to the "Gay Vote" during the
mayoral elections in Boston, and the 1980 presidential campaign.

Lesbian and Gay Media Advocates

℅ GCN 22 Bromfield Street Boston,.Ma. 02108

Story Ideas
Page 4

Resources:

Gay Community News: 22 Bromfield Street, Boston, 02108; 426-4469.

Massachusetts Gay Political Caucas: 471-8404

III. ARTS AND CULTURE

General Goal:

The goal here is both for gay and lesbian readers to have their culture documented, as well as for all readers to know of the substantial and diverse things it has to offer.

Specific Story Ideas:

1) An article or a series on the growth of women's culture (a significant part of which is lesbian) - novels, poetry, music. This could include reviews of all-women's concerts (like Alix Dobkin's, or Teresa Trull's recent concerts); an article about the Michigan Women's Music Festival which happens each summer and is well attended by Boston women; an article about the standard rule of having signers for the hearing-impaired at all women's events.

2) Articles attempting to convey an understanding of both the diverse and specific elements if the artistic and literary history of gay and lesbian culture. Is there such a thing as a gay aesthetic?

3) An article on the numerous women's production companies in the area.

4) An article about Glad Day Bookstore, New Words Bookstore, Artemis, Iris Film Productions.

Resources:

Area newspapers such as the Gay Community News, Sojourner's, and Equal Times (426-1981) provide good cultural listings of relevant events.

Thank you for your attention to these concerns. We hope this listing has been helpful, and encourage you to contact us should you have any questions or comments.

Diane Greene
Urvashi Vaid
for LAGMA

Appendix 3:

Style Guidelines

These are guidelines we've proposed that the press adopt for coverage of lesbian and gay issues. You are welcome to copy them directly, or to revise them to meet your particular needs.

Avowed homosexual: Use of the word "avowed" in this context is as unnecessary as saying "avowed Catholic" or "avowed Caucasian" and it creates a clearly negative bias. When a person's sexual orientation is appropriate to a story it can be handled very simply: "John Doe, a gay man,..." or "Mary Jones, a lesbian activist,..."

Fag, Dyke, etc.: There are times when it is appropriate to quote someone (a public official, for example) as using the word "nigger" and there are times when it is appropriate to quote someone saying "fag" or "dyke". But there aren't many such times and the same criteria should be used in each case. Ditto for derogatory or stereotyped phrases, from "cheap Jew" to "leering lesbian".

Gay rights: This term may imply to readers that gay and lesbian activists are asking for special rights and privileges. Generally gays are seeking only the civil rights protection that other minorities have sought; the phrase "gay civil rights" thus more clearly reflects the real concerns of this movement than does "gay rights".

Gay women: In principle, a social group should be identified by the name that its members prefer. There is no Harris poll on the subject, but the term "lesbian" seems to be increasingly preferred over "gay women".

Homosexual: This word refers to both sexes, but most readers, on seeing it, will think strictly of male homosexuals. If that's the meaning you intend, it should be spelled out: "gay men" or "homosexual men". If you mean to include both sexes, readers are more likely to understand you if you use a term such as "gay people", "gay men and women" or "lesbians and gay men".

Homosexual rape, homosexual murder, etc.: If a violent crime involves a homosexual or heterosexual act, that fact will generally be clear from the facts presented in the story. The sexual element of the crime can be spelled out, but it is highly prejudicial and inflammatory to use a term such as "homosexual murder" unless you also, whenever the facts so warrant, refer to "heterosexual murder".

"Homosexuals, drug addicts and derelicts" and similar phrases: In describing everything from a neighborhood to a social era, phrases like the one above are sometimes used by a writer to indicate that it's a bad one. It is unacceptable to include homosexuals in a list of negative attributes like this.

Letters to the editor, signed columns, etc.: In these areas, individual writers have a certain amount of latitude to express controversial opinions. Bigoted and prejudicial opinions and phrases about lesbians and gay men should be accepted or rejected for publication based on the same standards as if the comments were directed at racial, ethnic or religious minorities.

Sexual preference: Most authorities agree that a person's sexuality (heterosexual/homosexual) has been determined by a very young age and, as a rule, can be hidden but not changed in later life. "Sexual orientation" is thus a more accurate term than "sexual preference" or "sexual choice".

Stereotypes: In covering an event such as a lesbian and gay pride march, it is tempting to focus on the participants who are dressed in the most unusual costumes. At the Republican National Convention it might be okay to focus on the fellow wearing a papier-mache elephant on his head; everybody knows that not all Republicans dress like that. But in the case of lesbians and gay men, many stereotyped images exist. It is our responsibility in such a case to give our readers an accurate and representative image of the marchers.

Appendix 4:

Questions You'll Hear at a Meeting With the Media

Whenever we've met with media representatives, certain questions inevitably come up again and again. Here are some of the points we've made in answer to these questions; plan ahead of time how you will reply to them.

Why do you use the word "gay"?
• It's less clinical-sounding than "homosexual".
• A group has a right to select a term for themselves; i.e. blacks, Native-Americans, Hispanics, etc.
• Avoid an intellectual discussion of the *origin* of the word "gay". The point is, it has been chosen by us and should be respected.

How are homosexuals actually discriminated against?
• Civil rights laws usually do not protect against discrimination based on sexual orientation. Thus even if a landlord actually says, "I don't want queers living here," you have no recourse.
• Mention any legislation that is pending, or that has passed, that affects you in this regard. In 1982, for example, the proposed "Family Protection Act" specifically legislates against gay civil rights.
• Lesbians often lose their children in custody suits.

• Many lesbians and gay men face almost certain loss of their job if it becomes known that they are gay — e.g. teachers, military personnel, public office holders, etc. Most of us have no protection against being fired by a homophobic employer.

• Also see replies for next question.

You talk about being an "oppressed minority" — how are you oppressed?

• Give personal examples here: what it's like to have to drop your lover's hand in public; to feel uncomfortable having your loved one's picture out on your desk; to listen to co-workers tell "fag jokes" at lunch.

• Note that there is much documentation of "queer bashing" and probably most of it is unreported. Note incidents of verbal and physical abuse of gays by police.

• Point out that many people close the door on anyone who is openly gay or lesbian. Perhaps you know of a gay and lesbian student organization at a university that was denied access to buildings, funding or formal recognition. Or a gay bookstore or coffeehouse or newspaper that was unable to lease space because of discriminatory attitudes.

• Ask how *they* feel about gay men and lesbians. What do they think when they hear the word "homosexual"? Do they think that they discriminate?

Isn't it a private matter? Why do you have to come out and tell people you are gay? What people do in their bedrooms is their business, so why does it have to be a public issue? In short, why do you have to flaunt it?

• *Heterosexuals* go public all the time: with their wedding rings, their family pictures on the desk, holding hands and kissing in public. Heterosexuals routinely talk about what they did last week-end with their wives or husbands, girlfriends or boyfriends. Gay men and lesbians like to feel comfortable doing these things too. Why should we make a special effort to be secretive about our lives?

• We are talking *not* just about sexual orientation, but

about affectional orientation — not just about "what we do in bed" but our relationships, our right to love and care for one another.

Why do you always talk about it? Why do you have groups that just sit around to talk about it?
• As with other minorities that experience stigmatization, the group provides an indispensable opportunity for peer support, positive role models, consciousness raising, and encouragement to continue the struggle.

How can you claim to be a minority? After all, if it's sexual choice, then you could choose to not be homosexual.
• "Sexual choice" and "sexual preference" are not accurate terms; "sexual orientation" is more appropriate.
• Most studies agree that one's sexual and affectional orientation is established early in life, although a same-sex orientation is often *suppressed* for many years. Ask the heterosexuals whether they think they could *choose* to stop loving and relating to the opposite sex if society were to condemn *hetero*sexuality.
• If a member of a racial minority asks this question, avoid the "who's more discriminated against" argument. Try to align with the anger one feels at the discrimination.

What is the cause of homosexuality?
• The cause of homosexuality is as undefined as the cause of heterosexuality. You could briefly repeat that sexual orientation, whatever its cause, seems to be determined by early childhood.
• Try to avoid getting sidetracked with a long discussion of this issue.

Appendix 5:

A Press Advisory

Several years ago, the Suffolk County (Boston) District Attorney's office announced that they had broken a gay sex ring involving child pornography and boys being sold and exchanged for sexual purposes. Although it eventually became clear that no such ring ever existed, the local media had a field day with the story for many weeks. A group called the Boston/Boise Committee was formed in order to combat this sensationalism; what follows is a slightly modified version of the advisory that they issued to the press.

BOSTON/BOISE COMMITTEE, Box 277, Boston, MA 02123

SUGGESTIONS FOR MEDIA ON HANDLING ALLEGED SEX "CRIMES" INVOLVING GAY MEN

Grave errors, outright falsehoods and extreme sensationalism characterized much of the recent Boston media coverage of charges made by police against 24 men accused of sex with adolescent boys. The coverage amounted to trial by media and the bitter atmosphere of public outrage generated by the coverage would have been appropriate to a brutal murder case, certainly not to cases in which no violence or coercion was alleged. Many of the men and some of the "victims" suffered threats, loss of employment, loss of all social support from neighbors and friends and general harassment as a result of the coverage. Other gay men, although not involved, were also subjected to the homophobia of the community as a result of the "public outcry" which the District Attorney noted had been generated by the media reporting of the cases.

We urge each newspaper, radio station and television station in Greater Boston to voluntarily adopt the following suggestions as rational guidelines to protect the civil rights of everyone involved and to uphold the integrity of responsible journalism in reporting sex cases that allegedly involve gay men. While these views are made from the perspective of the gay male community, some of them will apply to heterosexual or lesbian situations as well. In any case, the suggestions are for *cases where violence is not involved and where evidence is frequently based on emotional testimony*. Especially in such cases, persons must be given every possible chance to exonerate themselves before being judged guilty.

SPECIFIC SUGGESTIONS
A. Safeguards for the rights of defendants and victims. (Both are likely to be real victims in a variety of ways.)

1. Do not publish the addresses or exact employment of the accused. Do not emphasize personal data that has no proven relationship to the "crime," but which might be linked by biased readers, such as Boy Scout work, foster parenthood, etc. Do not publish the photographs of persons accused of such "crimes," unless they volunteer to be photographed. Such safeguards are far more necessary in these cases than in the case of other "crimes" because of the general homophobia in some segments of the population which often leads to irrational and vicious personal attacks, violence, and malicious gossip.

2. Do not publish phone numbers of police "hotlines" which call for anonymous or other general tips concerning sex among men or among men and boys. Insist that the police requests for publicity be limited to cases at hand and that such public calls for action include warnings against gossip, hysteria and guilt by association.

3. Do not publish police "leaks" or other unproven statements about impending arrests of unnamed men who may be prominent ministers, social workers, foster parents, or politicians. "Tip-of-the-iceberg" comments by detectives and district attorneys should be recognized as politically motivated and fear-mongering. They are usually without merit (as such statements in these cases have proven to be without merit) and they have a chilling effect on the rights of all gay men, especially those legitimately involved with youth in their work or personal lives.

4. Do not describe the "victims" in such a way that they may be readily identified by peers. Ask police how the "victims" have been questioned and whether they are now in police custody. If so, ask to interview them to determine whether their rights and needs have been served. Specifically, inquire whether they have been provided genuinely neutral legal counsel and psychological aid.

5. Give equal space and prominence to stories that deal with alleged police harassment or mishandling of such cases and to stories that give the other side — that is, stories showing evidence of likely innocence. Give particular prominence to cases where serious errors have been revealed in the original stories or where cases have been dropped for lack of evidence. Persons accused of rape in front-page headlines deserve more than tiny back-page retractions.

B. *A responsible approch to investigative reporting.*

1. Avoid yellow journalism style and use of obviously biased words such as "prey," "sex den," "sordid."

2. Use of the term "homosexual" or "gay" as an adjective modifying "sex crime," "sex case," "prostitution," and other similar words is unnecessary and prejudicial. Similar "heterosexual" cases are not so identified.

3. Be sensitive to the tremendous homophobia in our soceity. Do not pander to it more than one would pander to racism or other extreme prejudices.

4. Ask direct questions of police, bureaucrats and elected officials involved in the case. Such persons sometimes depend on sensationalism, including charges later modified or dropped or juicy details which never have to be proven in order to get media mileage.

5. Do not publish statements of "unnamed detectives" or other unidentified sources without checking them out. They may be politically motivated or stem from the personal homophobia of these persons. This is especially true for details which will never have to be proven in court, but which damage the reputation of the accused. This is particularly true when the unnamed source is, in turn, quoting a third party who cannot deny or verify the statement.

6. Insist on seeing the indictments in order to be precise about the nature of the accusations. Only the sloppiest journalism

could have linked 24 cases with "child pornography" when no such accusation was made!

7. Do not fall into the police-laid trap of linking unlinked "crimes" simply because they are *announced* to the media at the same time. This is the worst form of guilt by association. It is also the misuse of the media by district attorneys and others to further their careers.

8. Ask authorities the nature of the investigation, the nature and timing of questioning of witnesses, and the sources of the complaints: the "victims," their peers, their parents, neighbors, known prostitutes, police.

9. Insist on precise information about the ages of the victims and the dates of the alleged acts. Be precise in the use of age terms like "children," certainly not appropiate when used for a person who was 15 at the time of the alleged act and now who is 22.

C. *A clear and informative description of the alleged offense.*

1. Clearly differentiate among the types of alleged offenses, explaining to the public the complicated terminology of these.

a. "Rape and Abuse of a Child" does not involve force, violence or any form of coercion. In heterosexual cases, it is always specifically referred to as *statutory* rape, and it should be so identified with regard to homosexual cases. "Child" is defined variously as under 14 or under 16 or under 18.

b. "Forcible Rape" which involves violence or coercion is extremely rare among gay men and adolescents — remember that adolescent boys are usually as strong as or stronger than adult men — but it should be identified as such when the accusation has been made.

c. "Intent to Rape" does not have to involve even touching the alleged victim — "erotic intent" is enough!

d. Statutory rape of a male minor does NOT have to involve penetration of the mouth or anus of either partner — touching is sufficient if perceived by a witness to be sexual in nature. Such cases invite the broadest hysteria and homophobic reactions. A boy mowing the lawn of a gay male couple may enter the house for a lemonade and the parents could bring charges that would be sufficient to prosecute on the assumption of intent to rape.

e."Prostitution" and "Soliciting" are vigorously prosecuted among women, while their customers usually go free (and unnamed). The opposite is often the case among gay men and boys, where the client is prosecuted and the prostitute is coerced into state testimony.

f. "Lewd and Lascivious Acts," "The Unnatural and Unmentionable Act," "Contributing to the Delinquency of a Minor," etc., are similarly vague and need explanations. The public shoud be informed that a person may be charged for *each single act* alleged and that the *same* act may be prosecuted as all of the above "crimes" (except forcible rape), so that one man accused of several similar acts with one teenaged boy might face 100 life sentences.

2. Indicate the heavy possible penalties for the alleged crimes: life imprisonment is possible for several of the above, and 5–10 years is often the minimum sentence. Anyone serving any sentence for any of these crimes may be judged a "sexually dangerous person" by court-appointed psychiatrists and then may be held for from one year to life, or until he is ruled no longer dangerous.

3. "Prostitution Rings" are not the same as individual hustling, and neither necessarily involve "child molestation" or "child pornography." Be precise and correct in headlines, captions, summaries and all other descriptions of the behavior of the alleged violators.

D. *Independent verification of news.*
1. Before printing stories of this kind on a major scale and solely on police evidence, several diverse sources should be checked to verify that the charges have some merit, and several gay sources should be contacted for a reaction to the tone of the story. No one person speaks for our community.

Lesbians and gay men have their own media and other institutions. We are a diverse group, but WE ARE AN IMPORTANT COMMUNITY within a larger Boston society. Some of us are consumers of products you advertise, most of us see your media, and a few of us contribute to your media or work for you. We can and will use all available power in common self-interest if the media are not reponsive to these reasonable suggestions. We will not tolerate erroneous charges and the damaging impact of such sensationalism upon our bothers and sisters. Our Boston/Boise Committee is made up of nearly 120 gay and straight men and women including working people of all ages and professions. We also include representatives from such major organizations as Metropolitan Community Church, *Gay Community News*, *Fag Rag*, Homophile Community Health Service, Dignity, the Libertarian Party and the Civil Liberties Union. We are united in our anger that the rights of the 24 recent defendants and their alleged "victims" have been irreparably harmed and that shocking misrepresentations by the media have made fair trials in these cases unlikely if not impossible. We call upon you in fairness and for the sake of professional integrity to follow these suggestions so that such wrong will not be done again.

Please sign and check one of the following:

1. As an individual media person, I agree to follow the above suggestions.

_____

2. Our organization (Name: _____)
will follow the above suggesions.

3. We make the following further suggestions:

Signed: _____
    Media:
    Date:

Appendix 6:

Addresses

MEDIA-WATCHERS:

Columbia Journalism Review: Columbia University, Graduate School of Journalism, 700 Journalism Bldg., New York, NY 10027.

Federal Communications Commission: 1919 M St. NW, Washington, DC 20054. 202-632-6336. Also check your local phone book for office nearest you.

National News Council: 1 Lincoln Plaza, New York, NY 10023. 212-595-9411.

MAGAZINES:

Newsweek: 444 Madison Ave., New York, NY 10022. 212-350-2000.

Time: Time & Life Building, New York, NY 10020. 212-586-1212.

U.S. News and World Report: 2300 N St. NW, Washington, DC 20037. 202-861-2000.

BROADCAST MEDIA:

American Broadcasting Companies (ABC): 1130 Avenue of the Americas, New York, NY 10019. 212-887-7777.

CBS: 51 W. 52 St., New York, NY 10019. 212-975-4321.

Mutual Broadcasting System: 1755 S. Jefferson Davis Hwy., Arlington, VA 22202. 703-685-2000.

National Broadcasting Co. (NBC): 30 Rockefeller Plaza, New York, NY 10020. 212-664-4444.

WIRE SERVICES AND SYNDICATES:

Associated Press (AP): 50 Rockefeller Plaza, New York, NY 10020. 212-621-1500.

United Press International (UPI): 220 E. 42nd St., New York, NY 10017. 212-682-0400.

United Feature Syndicate: 200 Park Ave., New York, NY 10166. 212-557-2333.

Additional addresses:

Use the space below to write in addresses and phone numbers of the newspapers, magazines, TV and radio stations that you most often read, watch and listen to. You can also use this space to keep track of who you talk to when you call each of these places; by asking for that same person the next time you'll begin to build a valuable network of personal contacts in the media.

More addresses:

More addresses:

OTHER ALYSON BOOKS YOU WILL ENJOY

Don't miss our **free book** offer at the end of this section!

REFLECTIONS OF A ROCK LOBSTER*
A story about growing up gay
by Aaron Fricke; $4.95

No one in Cumberland, Rhode Island was surprised when Aaron Fricke showed up at his high school prom with a male date; he had sued his school for the right to do so, and the papers had been full of the news ever since. Yet until his senior year, there would have been nothing to distinguish Aaron Fricke from anyone else his age. You'd never have guessed he was gay — and Aaron did his best to keep it that way. He created a shell around himself as protection against a world that he knew would reject him if it knew the truth. But finally his anger became too great, and he decided to make a stand.

Now, in *Reflections of a Rock Lobster*, you can read Fricke's moving story about growing up gay — about coming to terms with being different, and a lesson in what gay pride can really mean in a small New England town.

BETWEEN FRIENDS
by Gillian E. Hanscombe; $5.95

Lillian Faderman, author of *Surpassing the Love of Men*, writes that "*Between Friends* is an achievement. [The author explores] many of the vital lesbian and feminist issues of our day — monogamy, communal living, living with men, sexual relations with men, racism, lesbian motherhood, boy children in the lesbian community, the place of love in a radical movement. She succeeds both in involving the readers in the emotional lives of her characters and demanding of the readers a serious re-examination of their beliefs about the sorts of lives lesbians and feminists ought to be living."

Asterisked titles are copublished with, or distributed by, Gay Men's Press, PO Box 247, London N15 6RW, England.

YOUNG, GAY AND PROUD!*
edited by Sasha Alyson; $2.95

One high school student in ten is gay. Here is the first book ever to address the problems and needs of that often-invisible minority. It helps young people deal with questions like: Am I really gay? What would my friends think if I told them? Should I tell my parents? Does anybody else feel the way I do?

ROCKING THE CRADLE
Lesbian mothers: A challenge in family living
by Gillian E. Hanscombe and Jackie Forster; $5.95

Lesbian mothers are often in the news these days, but usually they get just superficial treatment, triggered by child custody cases. Here is the first book to thoroughly look at topics such as the social and personal aspects of lesbian motherhood; the implications of AID (artificial insemination by donor); and how children feel about growing up with lesbian mothers.

Both authors have long been active in the lesbian movement, but their book assumes no special knowledge or experience on the part of the reader. *Rocking the Cradle* discusses questions ranging from the most basic to the most specific, from "What is a lesbian?" to "How can women administer AID on their own?"; all in a style that is clear and thought-provoking.

THE ADVOCATE GUIDE TO GAY HEALTH *
R. D. Fenwick; $6.95

You'd expect a good gay health book to cover a wide range of information, and this one does. What you wouldn't expect is that it could be so enjoyable to read! Here you'll find the expected information about sexually-transmitted diseases;

you'll also learn about such things as what you should know before going into sex therapy; how some lesbians and gay men have handled their fear about aging; and the important lessons of the holistic health movement.

THE MEN WITH THE PINK TRIANGLE*
by Heinz Heger, $4.95

Here is the true story of a chapter in gay history that has long been hidden from view. In 1939, the author was a young medical student, in love with the son of a Nazi officer. In March of that year the Gestapo abruptly arrested him for homosexuality, and he spent the next six years in concentration camps. Like thousands of other homosexuals, he was forced to wear a pink triangle on his shirt so he could be readily identified for special abuses.

Richard Hall, book columnist for *The Advocate*, praised this as "One of the ten best books of the year" and *Gay Community News* warns that "You may find yourself riveted to your seat" by Heger's narrative.

THE AGE TABOO*
Gay male sexuality, power and consent
edited by Daniel Tsang; $5.95

Man/boy love is one of the most controversial issues ever to split the gay community. Here are a number of perspectives on the subject of intergenerational sex. The writers raise such broad-reaching questions as: What constitutes true consent? When does the "protection" of young people (or any other group) turn into their oppression? How do power differences affect personal relationships? It rapidly becomes clear from these essays that an understanding of the age taboo helps shed light on a great many aspects of human sexuality.

To get these books:

Ask at your favorite bookstore for the books listed here. You may also order by mail. Just fill out the coupon below, or use your own paper if you prefer not to cut up this book.

GET A FREE BOOK! When you order any two books listed here at the regular price, you may request a *free* copy of either *Talk Back!* or *Young, Gay and Proud!*

BOOKSTORES: Standard trade terms apply. Details and catalog available on request.

Send orders to: **Alyson Publications, Inc.**
PO Box 2783, Dept. B-10
Boston, MA 02208

— — — — — — — — — — — — — — — — — — — —

Enclosed is $_____ for the following books. (Add $.75 postage when ordering just one book; if you order two or more, we'll pay the postage.)

☐ The Age Taboo ($5.95)
☐ The Advocate Guide to Gay Health ($6.95)
☐ Between Friends ($5.95)
☐ The Men With the Pink Triangle ($4.95)
☐ Reflections of a Rock Lobster ($4.95)
☐ Rocking the Cradle ($5.95)
☐ Talk Back! ($3.95)
☐ Young, Gay and Proud! ($2.95)
☐ Send a free copy of _____
as offered above. I have ordered at least two other books.

name: _____

address: _____

city: _____ state: _____ zip: _____

ALYSON PUBLICATIONS
PO Box 2783, Dept. B-10, Boston, Mass. 02208